HERB
cookery

and other recipes
by alan hooker

illustrated by
linda robertson

edited by
helen morrow

published by
101 productions
san francisco

Third Printing, May, 1973

Distributed to the Book Trade
in the United States of America
by Charles Scribner's Sons, New York

Distributed in Canada by
Van Nostrand Reinhold, Ltd., Scarborough, Ontario

Published by
101 PRODUCTIONS
834 Mission Street
San Francisco, California 94103

contents

 Many recipes in this book call for special herb blends and herb salt. These are marked with an asterisk. The ingredients for the various blends will be found on pages 10 and 11.

introduction

In embarking on another book of recipes created at the Ranch House it seems worthwhile to make this one explanatory about the use of herbs and spices.

As I wrote in "Vegetarian Gourmet Cookery," I began to rely on herbs because it was apparent how necessary they were to add flavor to vegetarian cooking. Naturally, this is equally true of cooking meat, fish and fowl.

This wonderful source of delicious flavors has been neglected by too many people. Because of an increased awareness everywhere about food preparation this is an appropriate time to write about the great variety of herbs and spices that are so easily available, both fresh and dried.

The meat and fish recipes in this book were developed during the period when we changed the Ranch House from a vegetarian restaurant to one with a full menu. In this interval I had to eat meat, but since then I have returned to the vegetarian diet.

This is not just a book about herbs and spices, however, it is a recipe book concerned with basic foods first and how they are enhanced by the judicious use of herbs and spices. A few recipes do not even have herbs or spices, but they are so good they should not be excluded.

If possible, grow a few herbs yourself for it is not difficult and does not take much space in the garden or on a sunny kitchen window ledge.

Alan Hooker

5

herbs and spices

This is not an herb book revealing arcane information about the subject. It is fundamentally a cookbook in which the recipes call for herbs and spices to give their special flavors to the food. Only such details are given as will prove useful to the cook in preparing the dish, and a few side remarks about such things as the wonders of nature. Because I am fundamentally a cook, I have focused my attention on the use rather than the theory of herbs in cooking.

My first knowing experience with herbs in food was like coming in the wrong door. This was many years ago. I was in Michigan on a lecture tour and my hostess, who raised herbs to sell, announced that we would have herbs in our dinner. We were both vegetarians and she had prepared some of those little gluten choplets one can buy in a can. She put one on my plate, covered with what appeared to be a mat of dried leaves. As this was my first experience I assumed that all was well. My first bite revealed the error of my assumption. In their dry state some herbs are sharp and some are bitter and some are thorny, to say the least, and she had put enough of them on my little choplet to flavor the food for ten people. I was polite and got through the meal somehow, but silently I made a vow never to touch herb cooking. Of course you know what such vows lead to.

The lesson in this experience for the beginner is to start experimenting with small amounts. Put a pinch of this or that in the pot and see what happens. Carefully follow tested recipes using herbs. Find out what most pleases your own taste, for that is the standard you must meet. No other person, no recipe can determine what tastes good to you.

GROWING YOUR OWN

The best place to grow herbs is in a small garden close to the kitchen. Human nature being what it is, when you have to run around the corner of the house for fresh herbs, you'll probably just reach for the bottle on the shelf containing dried ones. So, if possible, arrange it so you can reach out the kitchen door and pluck the sprigs you need. A three-by-three-foot area will be enough room.

The flavor in herbs and spices is contained in their essential oils. These are developed when the plant has to protect itself from excessive evaporation of its moisture through the leaves. It manufactures oil in the leaves for this purpose, and this oil has flavor.

When I had been in California just long enough to learn to identify its trees, I was driving up the coast along the Big Sur and discovered some bay trees with the longest leaves I had ever seen. I got out and picked some of them and took them home. Imagine my surprise when the leaf I put in the soup disintegrated, leaving only some little sharp pieces that stuck in the throat. On a walk into one of the canyons around Ojai I again found bay trees, but in this dry area the leaves were thick and tough and very, very fragrant. They had developed a tough hide and filled it with oil to stop the evaporation of their juices.

So it is with all herb plants. Select a good sunny place where the soil is not too rich. Plant your herbs with room to grow and don't water them too much, only enough to make them grow. A few herbs will need good soil, but let all of them struggle and make more oil for their survival. There is an exception, of course. Parsley needs good soil and plenty of water, but its flavor is strong enough without any struggle to develop it.

If you are an apartment dweller you can still have an herb garden, if you have a window where there is plenty of sun. Herb cooking has become popular and practically any nursery or even your supermarket will have window-box kits and every kind of aid to start you off.

herbs and spices

BUYING PLANTS & SEEDS

For those who want to expand their herb gardens or add rare types of herbs, here is a list of places you can write for catalogs:

For seeds:

Comstock Ferre & Company, Box 125, Wetherfield, Connecticut, 06109

Greene Herb Gardens, Greene, Rhode Island, 02827

Mail Box Seeds, Shirley Morgan, 2042 Encinal Avenue, Alameda, California, 94501

George W. Park Seed Company, Greenwood, South Carolina, 29647

For plants:

Bittersweet Hill Nurseries, Route 424, Davidsonville, Maryland, 21035

Elbert Flower, 1879 Larking Rd., Boothwyn, Pennsylvania, 19061

The Herb Farm, Barnard Road, Granville, Massachusetts, 01034

Merry Gardens, Box 595, Camden, Maine, 04843

Smirz's Herb Nursery, 5573 Northridge, Route 20, Madison, Ohio, 44057

Sunnybrook Farm Nursery, 9448 Maryfield Road, Chesterland, Ohio, 44026

Pine Hills Herb Farm, Box 307, Roswell, Georgia, 30075

Taylor's Garden, 2649 Stingle Ave., Rosemead, California, 92770

Tool Shed Herb Farm, Purdy's Station, New York, 10578

Waynefield Herbs, 837 Cosgrove Street, Port Townsend, Washington, 98368

Well-Sweep Herb Farm, Mount Bethel Road, Port Murray, New Jersey, 07865

The Yarb Patch, 3726 Thomasville Road, Tallahassee, Florida, 32303

BUYING HERBS

If you cannot grow your own herbs, here are sources for buying them.

House of Herbs, 459 — 18th Avenue, Newark, New Jersey, 07108 (They have an extensive catalog of both culinary and medicinal herbs.)

Calumet Herb Company, Box 248, South Holland, Illinois, 60473. (This company has a fine list of botanicals.)

Nature's Herb Company, 281 Ellis Street, San Francisco, California, 94102

Tatra Herb Company, Box 60, 222 Grove Street, Morrisville, Pennsylvania 19067 (Foreign and domestic herbs and herb teas.)

Meadow Brook Herb Garden, Route 138, Wyoming, Rhode Island, 02898

Herbs, Box 266, Avis, Pennsylvania, 17721

Botanical Research Laboratory, Box 331, Chicago, Illinois, 60690

Indiana Botanic Gardens, Box 5, Hammond, Indiana, 46325

Penn Herb Company, 603 North Second Street, Philadelphia, Pennsylvania, 19123

Study these fascinating catalogs. There are herb teas, made from both leaves and roots, teas to help you sleep, to soothe your nerves, to settle your stomach, to curb your appetite. There are medicinal herbs—a lifetime study! Consider the ubiquitous comfrey, which according to some herbalists is supposed to cure almost anything.

STORAGE OF HERBS AND SPICES

I repeat, because it is so important: the flavor in herbs and spices is in their oils. These oils will evaporate, leaving you with only tasteless, stale or bitter husks. Time, light and heat are the agents that act to deplete these precious oils. Use up your herbs and spices; don't keep them around too long. Store them in tightly stopped bottles away from sunlight and heat. How many times have you seen an attractively decorated kitchen, with a spice shelf hanging over the stove, or near it, as part of the decor?

Science keeps discovering more curative properties and nutrients in herbs. With the judicious use of them in cooking one gets all this and wonderful flavor, too. So it is worthwhile to give them good care. Several magazines, Sunset, Better Homes and Gardens and House Beautiful have published practical plans for herb and spice storage. Write and ask them for information.

herbs and spices

HERB BLENDS

When you have made your herb garden, you will want to blend the ones you dry. Here are suggestions; you may want to change or add to them. Certain foods, however, almost demand certain herbs, such as: pork—sage; tomato or cheese—basil; fish—fennel; lamb—rosemary.

The following mixtures are given in proportions so that they can be made up ahead of time and stored.

For Soups

2 parts each: thyme or summer savory, parsley, chervil, basil, sweet marjoram, celery or lovage leaves.
1 part each: sage, rosemary, dried ground lemon peel.

For Salads

4 parts each: marjoram, basil, tarragon, parsley, chervil, celery, chives.
1 part each: lemon thyme, summer savory, costmary.

For Vegetables

1 part each: marjoram, basil, chervil, parsley, chives.
Pinch of: savory, thyme.

For Eggs

3 parts parsley.
1 part each: chervil, marjoram, tarragon, basil, chives.

For Fish

1 part each: tarragon, basil, marjoram, chervil, parsley.

For Chicken and Veal

4 parts each: marjoram, basil, chervil, parsley.
1 part each: thyme, lemon verbena.

For Beef

1 part each: marjoram, basil, parsley, lovage or celery leaves.
Large pinch of summer savory, thyme.

Savory Herbs

1 part each: basil, marjoram, celery tops, parsley, costmary, tarragon.
Pinch of: savory, thyme.

For Lamb

4 parts each: marjoram, basil, parsley.
1 part each: rosemary, savory.

For Pork

1 part each: pineapple sage (or regular sage), basil, marjoram, summer savory.

For Poultry Stuffing

1 part each: marjoram, sage, basil, parsley, savory, celery leaves, dried ground lemon peel.

For Tomatoes

1 part summer savory.
4 parts each: thyme, parsley, marjoram, basil.

RANCH HOUSE HERB KIT

Because so many guests at the Ranch House asked us for the herb blends we put into various dishes, we have made up a kit containing seven of these blends and some of our herb salt. Write for a descriptive folder.
Address: The Ranch House, Ojai, California, 93023.

herbs and spices

THE BOUQUET GARNI

When using fresh herbs, you may want to make a bouquet of the sprigs and tie them together with a string or in a cheesecloth bag so that they can be removed when the food is cooked.
A basic bouquet is:
2 sprigs parsley
1 sprig marjoram
1 sprig basil
1 sprig thyme
There are innumerable variations. You could add one sprig of any of these: tarragon, summer savory, dill, costmary, pineapple sage; or a sprig of each of two or more. Put a bouquet in your next pot of soup. A nice suggestion: Take to a sick friend a little bouquet of fresh, fragrant herbs. It will lift the ailing spirit and help to clear the air.

HERB SALT

Blend your own! Start with:
1 teaspoon garlic salt
2 teaspoons onion salt
1 teaspoon dry parsley
Next time, add to the above:
1/2 teaspoon basil
1/2 teaspoon marjoram
These two herbs are mild; you might like to add:
thyme or mint, a small pinch
(Careful, don't overdo it!)
This way you will soon learn the strength of each herb and see for yourself what you like and how much of it to use. It can be great fun.

To release the flavors of the herbs you are going to add to a dish, grind them in the mortar with the salt or herb salt. This blends them before they go into the mixture. You can do this with dry or fresh herbs.

SESAME SALT

Put into a frying pan and heat gently until the seeds begin to brown; do not overheat:
8 parts raw sesame seeds
1 part sea salt (available at health food stores)
Remove and allow to cool, then put into the blender a little at a time and run until well mixed. It is not supposed to be completely smooth; many of the seeds should still be whole. Sprinkle this on foods at the table—soups, salads, entrees— but when you do this, don't use too much salt in cooking. This mixture gives wonderful texture and flavor.

herbs and spices

DESSERT SPICE BLEND

The traditional spices most
widely used are cinnamon, nutmeg,
cloves, allspice and ginger, in
the order given. You can put them
all together in a blend that does
not have one overbalancing flavor!
2 teaspoons powdered cinnamon
2 teaspoons ground nutmeg
1 teaspoon powdered ginger
1/2 teaspoon powdered allspice
1/4 teaspoon powdered cloves
Mix them ahead of time and use
the mixture in spice cakes,
cookies and pies with delightful
results.

For extra-special pastry
concoctions, you can enlarge on
this by adding a few of the more
unusual spices such as:
1/2 teaspoon mace
1/2 teaspoon ground coriander
1/2 teaspoon ground cardamon

FAR EASTERN SPICE BLENDS

If you use other spices, beyond
those above, you will be going in
the direction of the exotic East.
Thus for Western tastes proceed
with caution, but proceed!
One of the foundations of good
curry powder is turmeric. Flavor
is then added with coriander,
cardamon, ginger and fenugreek.
Now comes the hot part: cumin
with its slightly bitter taste and
good pepper hotness; chilies of
many types, fresh or dried, green
or red, large and small;
and black peppercorns.
Pan-cooked vegetables (page 63)
give you a good chance to try out
spice combinations. Always
use small amounts of spices to
get the sense of their individual
flavors. You must educate
yourself. No one can teach you
about flavors; your own palate
will tell you all you need to
know. Trust it and it will
serve you well all of
your cooking life.

CURRY POWDER

In India, it is said, there are
as many varieties of curry powder
as there are cooks. Since anyone
who is interested in using herbs
and spices in cooking will want
to have at hand a good curry
powder, here is a chance to be
creative. Start off with a good
but simple blend.
Grind in the blender or with
mortar and pestle until powdery
fine:
6 tablespoons coriander seed
1/8 teaspoon cayenne pepper
1-1/2 tablespoons powdered
turmeric
1/2 tablespoon whole cloves
1-1/2 tablespoons fenugreek seed
1/2 tablespoon cardamon seed
1-1/2 tablespoons cumin seed
If you don't have a blender using
the mortar and pestle will make
a lot of work, but be sure and
pound the mixture well until it
is a fine powder.

THE VARIOUS HERBS AND SPICES

This is a cookbook using herbs and spices, not an herb book with recipes. Thus I have listed primarily those that are useful in cooking, plus a few household and medicinal uses for them. Many authorities classify herbs as the soft part of plants—their leaves and blossoms; spices the hard part—the seeds, bark, roots and kernels. Usually herbs are mild, spices are stronger. Experienced cooks may use a mixture of the two, but caution is necessary because the wrong combination can produce a small tragedy.

Allspice. So named because it combines the flavor of cinnamon, cloves and nutmeg, and hints of more. It is the dried and unripe fruit of the evergreen pimenta tree, that grows in Jamaica. Its subtle taste is found along with other flavorings in chutneys, pickles and ketchup. It combines happily even in sausage and poultry blends; and fruit cake or mince pie simply would not be what they are without it.

Angelica. Garden angelica or the herb of the angels was so named because it was supposed to have dispelled the plague and protected from harm all those who used its leaves. In France, it is candied and used for flavoring, as well as in many liqueurs such as anisette and Benedictine. All parts of the herb are aromatic; the leaves are especially good in fish dishes.

Anise. This is one of the oldest known herbs and was even praised by Pythagoras. The tops are very good in cooking if used sparingly. The licorice-flavored seeds, known as aniseed, may be used in pastries, soups and teas, and as a flavoring for candies and liqueurs. Mixed with lard, anise is said to relieve itching from insect bites.

Balm Lemon. These very hardy, intensely fragrant leaves are inclined to be bitter in cooking, but very useful combined with other herbs, such as borage, marjoram, thyme or basil.

Basil, Sweet. There are probably some sixty species of basil differing in height, color and taste, and it is one of the most widely used herbs known. The sweet and purple varieties are very common and essential in Italian cooking. Sweet basil has the capacity of sweetening foods like tomatoes. It is also used in vinegars, soups, salads (fresh), cottage cheese, egg dishes, meats, fish and chicken.

herbs and spices

Bay Leaf. Bay leaves may be used in all meat cooking, soups, vegetable cocktails and always in pickle spices. When boiling shrimp it is essential to put bay leaves in the water; they impart a subtle flavor which diminishes the fishy taste. In Europe the leaves are from the bay laurel tree; the California bay tree is a different variety. The ancient Greeks wove the bay laurel leaves into a wreath to crown their victorious warriors, thus the word laurel.

Borage. This plant produces beautiful blue flowers all summer. Its leaves are useful in fish, soups and salad dressing.

Burnet. This herb has the flavor of cucumber so that those who cannot eat cucumbers can use this instead. Its leaves are delightful in salads or iced drinks.

Capers. These plants grow wild along the mountainsides in Africa, Italy, France and Spain. The flower buds are gathered early in the morning before they open, and are pickled in vinegar and brine. Capers are a delicious addition to sauces, especially beef gravy, and to salads and canapés. They are used extensively in fish sauces.

Caraway. The seeds of this plant have many culinary uses. They are often used in cookies and breads, especially rye, and will add zest to cheeses, German sauerkraut and soups like clam chowder.

Cayenne and chilies. These are the hot red varieties of the enormous pepper family, the fruit of the tropical capsicum plant. There are said to be over 100 varieties of peppers, varying in size and flavor according to their species. The two most common types of chili pepper are the small Japanese chili which is extremely hot and should be used sparingly, and the larger Mexican chili which is much milder. Cayenne is the ground-up version of the red pepper and is an excellent addition to sauces, omelettes and ragouts.

Celery. In America we are not inclined to think of celery as an herb because it is so commonly served as a raw appetizer, especially in restaurants The seeds, salt and dried leaves, however, are used as a flavor ingredient quite extensively. Cut off the tops of celery, wash and dry the leaves, and then store them in a brown paper bag for use in seasoning soups and sauces. In the wild, celery is extremely bitter; even after cultivation it is considered a bitter herb and thus blends best with the bitter fowls like chicken and turkey, especially in stuffings and soup.

Chervil. This is used in all the French fines herbes blends and in the bouquet garni. Because its flavor is similar to celery, the two may be interchanged in recipes. Chopped fresh, it is excellent in tossed green salad, sauces like béarnaise or in butter sauce for chicken. Medicinally it has been used on bruises. In ages past, a drink made of ground chervil and wine was supposed to soothe the lungs.

Chicory. The roots are ground up and roasted to add a bitter taste to coffee such as is found in New Orleans. The leaves are the slightly bitter chicory lettuce used in salads. Propagation is by seed.

Chives. The chopped leaves impart a mild onion flavor to soups, cheese omelettes, fish and salads, making it essential to any kitchen garden.

Cilantro. This parsley-like plant, grown from coriander seeds is often called Spanish parsley, Chinese parsley, Hungarian parsley, etc., depending on the country where it is grown. (To add to the confusion, "Italian" parsley is a different variety altogether.) You should know how it looks, smells and tastes so that you can recognize it. Cilantro is short stemmed with thin, round, lightly fringed leaves. Both the smell and taste are quite pungent. Cilantro is easy to grow. Just get a package of coriander seeds from the grocery and plant them in a sunny location. Water generously and soon the little green shoots will appear. Cut the plant back after it has started branching and it will then send out more shoots. The leaves can be chopped and frozen in a sealed container. This way you will always have fresh cilantro; the frozen plant is just as good as the freshly picked. It does not dry well at all, because it loses its color and most of its fragrance. If you let it flower it will go to seed which can be dried and stored as coriander.

Cinnamon. Even the sound of the name of this most used spice is exotic. The best flavored cinnamon comes from Viet Nam, from the ground-up bark of the evergreen cassia trees. When the tree matures the bark is stripped from it, and the tree then dies. After each harvesting, new trees are planted and this cycle of harvesting and planting is maintained by the ceremonial planting of new trees, on all festive occasions. True cinnamon (not the cassia variety) is light brown in color, almost yellow, and much more delicate in flavor. Practically all of the cinnamon used in America is the stronger flavored cassia.

herbs and spices

Cloves. These are the unopened flower buds of one of the most beautiful of the evergreen trees, another of the cassia species. The Dutch name is kruidnagel, literally herb nail or spice nail; and the French call them clou, from the Latin clavus—nail. Cloves are used so much in canning, pickling, baking and so on because they bring such zest to the flavoring.

Coriander. The ground seeds are used in making curry powder and to flavor pastries, cheeses, vinegars and some sausages. A whole seed, freshly crushed, gives a cup of coffee an interesting flavor. English and Scotch candies were flavored with it years ago. The leaves are similar to parsley (see cilantro).

Costmary. The leaves, steeped fresh, are used mostly as a tea which is supposed to have curative powers as a tonic and nervine. This mild, sweet herb imparts a slight flavor of mint in cooking and is especially good in soups, sauces, chicken and fish dishes.

Cress (Overland Cress). Grown on land, this has a flavor similar to, but stronger than, watercress. It may be used in salads, soups, sauces and with chicken and fish, as well as in herb butters.

Cumin. In India, I am told, the whole seeds are used extensively in rice and curry dishes. In America, they are usually ground into a powder. Cumin is a basic ingredient of all prepared chili and curry powders. Its hotness and bitterness make its presence known whenever used, so add

it with caution. It can be blended sparingly with many soft cheeses and spaghetti sauce almost demands a touch of cumin.

Dill. Chopped dill leaves are a flavorful addition to fish, egg and cheese dishes, and to salads. The seeds are commonly used in pickling spices, as well as in apple pie, pastries, spiced beets, some soups, cabbage and sauerkraut. The Greeks believed dill to be so nourishing that athletes were required to eat it in all their food.

Fennel. The ancients said that snakes, which are especially fond of fennel, are made young again by this herb. In Europe the root is cooked as a vegetable. It may also be sliced raw in salads, grated into fish dishes, or brewed as a mild tea. Fennel tastes like anise, but its flavor is weaker.

Fenugreek. The seeds of this Eurasian plant are used primarily for making curry powder. It also makes an excellent tea which some say relieves nausea.

Flag (Sweet Flag). The roots are cut up and boiled in a syrup to flavor confections, custards and puddings. Also used in cough syrup.

Flax. The uses for flax are more medicinal than culinary. Boiled with grapefruit (see teas) it makes a drink which relieves colds. A mild laxative may be made by boiling the seeds in water, until a thick liquid is produced. To make a hot poultice, prepare a thick paste with the seeds and water and spread it on flannel.

Garlic. Need anyone ask about its use in cooking? Garlic is also purported to have many medicinal uses and, in the garden, is an insect repellent.

Geranium. There are some 75 varieties of fragrant leaf geraniums—apple, camphor, lemon, nutmeg, orange, almond, peppermint, licorice, rose, etc. These leaves give a wonderful fragrance to food, but they should be used with care and caution because they are some-times very pungent. To make an unusual salad dressing in the blender, add them sparingly; they may also be used in poultry stuffing. When making jelly, put one leaf in the bottom of the jar before filling it.

Ginger. Ginger root seems to have been used in cooking during all recorded time. It is native to tropical Asia and is available as a dry spice, used almost as much as cloves.
Who is not familiar with ginger bread and ginger ale? Fresh ginger root is becoming more readily available in American markets. Grated, it is an exotic addition to salad dressings, many meat and chicken dishes, and almost all Oriental cooking. The best ginger comes from Jamaica; it is also grown in Africa, India and the West Indies. The Chinese and Japanese roots are usually preserved for shipment here.

Horseradish. What would the English do without this to serve with their beef? It is also excellent mixed with mayonnaise. The root is ground and preserved in vinegar to prepare horseradish sauce. Always use white vinegar to keep the color white; cider vinegar will darken it.

Lavender. The seeds are used for cosmetics and perfumes. Place sprigs in linens to give them a wonderful aroma.

Leek. This is the sweetest member of the onion family. It can be steamed or braised and served as a vegetable, or cooked in soup (indispensable in vichysoisse).

Lovage. The plant looks like celery and has something of the same flavor. Thus in recipes calling for lovage, celery may be substituted. An excellent tea is made from the leaves. Propagation is by seed or by root division.

herbs and spices

Mace. This is the outer shell of the nutmeg kernel which has been ground and dried. It is stronger, however, than nutmeg. Mace is usually used in combination with other spices, but it is very good by itself when used to flavor cakes and cookies as well as sweet vegetables like carrots and new cabbage. Whipped cream and chocolate dishes are enhanced by its addition.

Marigold. (Pot marigold, calendula) The flowers of this plant have been used since the fifteenth century in France and England to flavor and color drinks. They may be added to soups, sparingly, used to color cheese, or in place of saffron.

Marjoram, Sweet. This, as well as basil, is one of the most useful sweet herbs. It can be used in all types of cooking, except desserts. Long ago it was used as a tea for nervous headaches.

Mint. The ancients believed that mint aroused latent passions, thus prohibited its use by military leaders, whom they wanted chaste. There are many varieties of mint—apple mint, corn mint, curly mint, variegated pineapple mint, caraway scented mint, orange bergamont mint, white peppermint, black peppermint, nutmeg scented mint, water mint and many others. It is very useful used sparingly with chicken or pork. An infusion makes wonderful tea, hot or cold. Mint sauce is made by boiling the leaves in a heavy sugar syrup and then discarding them.

Mustard seeds. Mustard seeds are used in all pickling spices and in making curry powder. In India, the black seeds are also used in cooking many different vegetables. We all know mustard sauce as an embellishment to the hamburger and other varieties of beef. But it's also a delicious addition to many cheese dishes,

especially cheese sandwiches. There are two varieties of mustard, the black and the white. Mustard leaves, steamed with other greens are a delicious vegetable.

Nasturtium. This plant is primarily grown for its beautiful flowers, but the leaves and stems are excellent in salads and the half-ripened seeds in pickles. Young nasturtium seeds may also be substituted for capers.

Nutmeg. This seed comes from an evergreen tree native to the Molucca Islands, although it is now grown in many other neighboring locales. The seed is dried and ground before using. Because the fragrant, pungent oil is volatile, it should be freshly grated whenever possible. Being not so strong as its close cousin, mace, it can be used more liberally in fruitcakes, pies and rolls. Nutmeg also enhances many cream sauces and soups, if used sparingly. It is especially good in custards and egg nogs.

herbs and spices

Onion. This bulb is unquestionably the most universal source of flavoring, a basic element in the cuisine of almost every country. Botanists, however, have never been able to establish its original home. Many cooks consider the large, flat white onion to be the strongest flavored of the cooking onions, with the yellow, red and Spanish or Bermuda onion less strong, in that order. The small white onions that are boiled and usually creamed are the mildest. The green onion has a variant that is a multiplier. It is very useful for it can be pulled like garlic and each segment planted to make more plants. Because of the penetrating power of the essence, onions are a wonderful catalyst in cooking.

Oregano (Wild Marjoram). There are many varieties of marjoram, but oregano is used more than any other in Italian, Spanish, Mexican and Greek cooking. Because oregano is very similar to, but much stronger than marjoram, the two are never used together. Although oregano may be substituted for marjoram if a stronger flavor is desired, the two are not always interchangeable. For example, when a deeper flavor is desired, as in tomato sauces, oregano is indispensable. In salads, oregano should be used very sparingly; sweet marjoram is preferable. The ancients believed that a drink made with ground oregano and white wine counteracted the poisons from snake and insect bites.

Paprika. In Hungary long ago a queen fell ill. Nothing helped her until a doctor prescribed paprika and she recovered. It was hailed as a magic herb and set off the Hungarian cooking spree that gave us all those delicious paprikash dishes, especially chicken. Paprika has been in good favor with cooks for centuries, and now modern science tells us it contains valuable vitamins and minerals. It is nice to know that this elegant red powder we have been cooking with and using as an attractive garnish is also very good nutritionally.

Parsley. Because of the near fetish of using parsley as a garnish we sometimes forget its most important values as a flavoring agent and a source of nutrition. Its acid-sweet pungency is a basic flavor in every bouquet garni. Nutritionists say that it has an amazing array of the animo acids that comprise the protein molecule. Thus it deserves a better culinary status than resting briefly on a plate of food and then being disgarded. Parsley is not only a seasoning; it can be used as a primary food ingredient, in soup, salad or deep-fried in clarified butter.

Pennyroyal. This herb makes an excellent tea with a mint flavor. For centuries it has been credited with repelling fleas when tied around a pet's neck.

Pepper, Black and White. Both come from the same peppercorns, only the black contains the whole corn; the more delicately flavored white pepper is used in sauces mainly because the black flecks would not be attractive in the sauce.

herbs and spices

Poppy Seeds. These are used in baking breads and cakes, and are also an interesting addition to sauces and salad dressing.

Rosemary. This is one of the oldest herbs known and is mentioned in all ancient writings about food. It is an excellent accompaniment to lamb and can be used sparingly with excellent results in salad dressings, stuffings, herb blends and stews. Rosemary is also used as a moth repellent and, when burned with juniper berries, as a disinfectant.

Rue. In cooking, care must be taken in the amount of this herb used. It may be added sparingly to vegetable cocktails, chicken dishes and stews.

Saffron. The tiny gold-colored stigmas of the crocus sativus plant are gathered with great patience in southern Europe and Asia; the Asian variety is darker and better flavored. Seventy-thousand hand-picked blossoms make a pound of true saffron. Now you know why it costs about $32 an ounce.

Sage. There are many different types of sage, but the most common variety used in cooking is garden sage. Others include pineapple, clary, meadow, black, dwarf and variegated sage. This herb, especially the pineapple variety, blends particularly well with pork dishes, stuffings and sausages. It also combines nicely with soft cheeses.

Savory. There are two distinct types of this herb—summer savory and winter savory. Both are very pungent and strong and should be used sparingly. The summer variety should be used in most recipes calling for savory, such as sauces, egg, fish and meat dishes. Winter savory, which is even more pungent, is the main ingredient used in frankfurters. The ancients claimed that savory mixed with wine prevented drowsiness; it was also said to be an aphrodisiac.

Sesame. The seeds, when roasted, are delicious on top of breads and rolls and added to some sauces. Sesame oil is one of the best and most universally used cooking oils. The dark roasted seeds make a pungent oil used as a seasoning in Chinese cooking. The ground up raw seeds make a product called tahini.

Sorrel. The tart French variety (sometimes called silver sorrel) is best for cooking. Garden sorrel is not so adapted to the kitchen. The culinary virtue of French sorrel, when added to dishes like French onion soup, is that it removes the undesired sweetness without adding a flavor of its own. It is often used in soups and salads for its tartness.

Shallot. This member of the onion family is grown extensively in Europe, but is sometimes difficult to find in America. Its distinctive flavor blends especially well with chicken and adds great interest to many soups and herb vinegars. It is essential to some sauces like béarnaise. If you cannot find shallots in your market, onions may be substituted with a pinch of garlic and sugar added.

Sunflower Seeds. The great and beautiful sunflower that Van Gogh painted so magnificently in the south of France provides a pleasant treat with its nourishing seeds. They are now available in all health food stores and in many supermarkets. Sunflower seeds can be used in many ways to add texture and nutrition to foods. They are an excellent addition to breads and loaf cakes. They are also especially good in combination with many vegetables that do not require much cooking; they will become too soft if overcooked. A bowl of the seeds placed on the coffee table is a fine substitute for the candy dish.

Tarragon, French. This herb is indispensible in the kitchen mélange of flavors. Who could imagine béarnaise sauce without it? I always add a bit of it also to scrambled eggs and freshly made mayonnaise. Tarragon is propagated by cuttings or by root division. Some find it difficult to grow; but if you have to buy or beg a large plant each spring, by all means add its enchantment to your cooking habits.

Thyme. Caraway, garden or lemon thyme, what variety do you wish? There is also silver, golden, woody, nutmeg, creeping moss, French and English thyme as well as many, many more. The English especially use thyme along their garden paths, so that when one walks on it the crushed herb gives off its delightful fragrance. The leaves of lemon thyme are particularly suited to fish and excellent in many sauces. The English and garden varieties may be used in all beef, lamb, poultry and pork dishes. Thyme is essential to every kitchen because of its ability to enhance combinations of herbs. Along with basil and sweet marjoram, it is basic to almost every herb blend.

Turmeric. This is an East Indian root that belongs to the ginger family. It is flint hard and must be ground to be used. It is not hot but is sharp and has a distinctive aroma and flavor.

Verbena, Lemon. This herb should always be used fresh; it loses its flavor when dried. The leaves are often used in fruit drinks, especially in champagne cocktails. To add an unusual flavor to pork or chicken dishes, lay the fresh leaves on top of the meat and bake or steam it in a covered pan. In times past, lemon verbena was used to make fragrant soaps. Its leaves placed between stored bed linen impart a wonderful fragrance. It is best propagated by cuttings.

Woodruff, Sweet. This is one of the sweetest smelling of the perennial herbs. The Germans use it to make their famous May wine and a sprig of it added to any cheap wine will make it palatable. It also imparts an unusual flavor to fruit punches.

herbs and spices

EQUIVALENTS

Fresh herbs are always preferable to the dried variety. City dwellers, however, sometimes find it difficult to obtain them. When converting measurements from fresh to dry herbs or the reverse, keep in mind that the dry herbs have had their essential oils concentrated in the drying process. Thus use them in smaller quantity. A good rule of thumb is:

2 sprigs of any fresh herb (top 2 inches of the new growth) equal about 1/8 teaspoon of the dried variety

This will vary slightly according to the age of the dry herb. They tend to lose their bouquet as the months pass and sometimes a slight bitterness develops with age.

Freshly ground pepper is also preferable. If you do not have a pepper mill follow this rule:

10 turns of the pepper mill equal approximately 1/4 teaspoon ground pepper

In following the recipes in this book, do not use ground herbs or spices unless specified. They are far more powerful than the whole variety.

Many writers have issued reams of material, a good part of it guesswork, regarding the development of sauces. Some say they were developed to disguise the fact that the food they dressed was not always fresh; others say sauces were invented to titillate the jaded palates of the high and mighty. Madame Pompadour, one reads, brought famous chefs from Italy to lend their magic to the cuisine at the French court. What does it matter? When you cook, delicious juices develop in the process and any imaginative cook is impelled to do something to them to enhance the dish. The great sauces concocted through the genius of creative chefs are our culinary heritage.

A sauce should never overpower the food it dresses but should complement its flavor, as a good béarnaise does on properly cooked beef or fish. Any gravy or liquid that develops in preparing food is a sauce, thickened or flavored with other things or not; and it should be handled carefully, for a poor sauce can ruin good food. For example, a perfectly cooked chicken can be ruined by a sauce which is cloudy or lumpy or too thick.

A French proverb says: "Frugality is the heart of good cooking." Never waste the juice from any food. In cooking, use only enough water to prevent burning, so that the liquid can be utilized for additional flavor. I cannot stress this too strongly; also, much of the mineral content of the food leaches out with the juice, so for health's sake, conserve it!

There are several ways that sauces can be thickened. A good agent to use is a mixture of tapioca flour and cornstarch in equal proportions, to which enough cold water has been added to make a thin paste. Add this to the sauce, stirring constantly, and the sauce will thicken. The value of this combination is that one ingredient works against the other: the starch keeps the tapioca from being gummy and the tapioca keeps the starch from being cloudy. The result is a sauce that actually has a sparkle to it. The mixture has greater thickening power than cornstarch alone, so slightly less should be used.

A paste of water and flour may also be used to thicken juices in which there is already some oil or fat, such as pan drippings. Liquids in which there is no fat may be thickened by the classic "roux" of butter and flour, in equal proportions. This may be kneaded together into a ball and added to the hot liquid, or blended together over low heat in a pan to which the hot liquid is added and then stirred with a whisk until thick.

23

sauces

BÉCHAMEL SAUCE

Heat, over very low heat, but do
not boil:
2 cups milk
1/2 bay leaf
(Remove bay leaf when milk is hot.
Heat in copper-bottom pan so milk
will not stick:
3 tablespoons butter
Blend well:
4 tablespoons flour
1-1/4 teaspoons herb salt*
pinch white pepper
Stir flour mixture into melted
butter slowly, until it makes
a thick paste, then slowly add to
heated milk stirring constantly
over low heat with a wire whisk
until thickened. Then add and
cook until thick:
1 egg yolk, mixed well in
2 tablespoons half-and-half cream
Remove mixture from fire
and add:
1-1/4 tablespoons sherry
(not dry)
Put small dots of butter on top
of sauce to prevent scumming.
Unless used immediately, cover
and refrigerate when cool.
Makes 3 cups

SAUCE MORNAY

The secret of this sauce is
the quality and age of the cheese.
It must be a strong variety such
as a good, very sharp Cheddar,
well aged. The aging process
breaks down the protein and
makes it possible for the
cheese to melt without getting
stringy. Kraft Cheddar,
packaged in the red-foil wrapper,
is very good and is available in
markets everywhere.
Prepare:
2 cups béchamel sauce, as in
preceding recipe
Add and mix in thoroughly on
low heat, stirring constantly to
blend all ingredients:
2 cups coffee cream
2 cups extra sharp cheddar,
grated fine
1 teaspoon Worcestershire sauce
1 additional tablespoon sherry
dash herb salt*
dash cayenne pepper
This sauce has so many uses that
a large amount can be made and
kept in the refrigerator for
at least a week without spoiling.
All that is necessary when you
want to use some is to put it
in a double boiler and reheat it.

HOLLANDAISE WITH
FRESH HERBS

Bring to a full boil, making sure
all the butter is melted:
1/2 pound butter
1/4 cup lemon juice, with enough
water added to make 2/3 cup liquid
2 sprigs tarragon
2 sprigs marjoram
2 sprigs lemon thyme
4 sprigs costmary
or 2 sprigs mint
1 sprig French sorrel
Heat blender with hot water.
Pour out water and put in:
3 egg yolks at room temperature
1/2 teaspoon gum tragacanth
(Optional, but it will help to keep
the sauce from separating.) Start
blender and immediately add
boiling butter mixture. Blend
only 10 or 15 seconds, no more,
or it will not thicken properly.
The beauty of this method of
making the sauce is that it is
quick and the sauce will hold up
on the warm element of an electric
stove or over hot water in
a double boiler for an hour before
serving. If it starts to separate
a few quick stirs with a wire
whisk will bring it together again.

BÉARNAISE SAUCE

Cook over high heat until reduced to 2/3 its original volume:
1 cup white wine
1 tablespoon tarragon vinegar
1 tablespoon shallots, chopped fine
(green onions may be used)
1 small sprig parsley, chopped fine
1 small sprig chervil (or
2 tablespoons celery tops, chopped fine)
2 small stalks tarragon
2 bruised peppercorns
When reduced, strain and return to pan, adding:
1/2 pound butter
Put into blender which has been heated with warm water:
3 egg yolks (at room temperature)

Heat butter and wine mixture until it begins to boil. Start blender whirling the egg yolks, and pour in immediately the wine and butter mixture. Whirl for about 10 seconds—just until it thickens; more will begin to thin it. If the butter and wine are not hot enough and the blender is not warm before the eggs go in, the sauce will not get thick; it is the slight cooking of the egg yolks that thickens it.
This sauce is best served at room temperature, which is the way Escoffier says it should be served. Do not try to serve it warm or it will separate. The present trend is to put meat glaze into it, which turns it gray, and then thicken it so it can be served warm. Horrible!

VARIATION OF MOUSSELINE SAUCE

The traditional mousseline sauce is made with a combination of hollandaise and whipped sweet cream. This variation has an interesting flavor, a bit more vital because of the reduced wine and herbs.
Whip just to lightness, not too thick:
sweet whipping cream
Fold it into the same amount of:
béarnaise sauce (at room temperature)
The sweet cream should be just firm enough to withstand the heaviness of the béarnaise.
Do not chill. This is a sauce for delicate foods like fresh filet of sole which has been only lightly fried in butter.

sauces

SAUCE FOR SWISS CHARD, BROCCOLI, ETC.

Grind together:
2 leaves costmary
2 sprigs thyme
2 leaves French sorrel (no stems)
2 large leaves lovage
1/4 teaspoon herb salt*
Mix with the herbs and cook until slightly thick:
1 cup water
2 tablespoons cornstarch dissolved in a little of the water
2 vegetable or beef cubes
1/4 cup yogurt
1/4 cup coffee cream
Add and stir in well:
2 tablespoons strong horseradish
Reheat to serving temperature. This sauce is excellent on all strong-flavored vegetables.

CREAMED HORSERADISH SAUCE

Whip until stiff but not buttery:
1/2 pint whipping cream
3/8 teaspoon gum tragacanth
(This stabilizes the sauce so it will not get soft.)
Add and fold in gently:
4 tablespoons strong horseradish
(Be sure you use the type that says strong on the label.)
1/4 teaspoon lemon juice
3/8 teaspoon herb salt*
This is good on any type of beef, especially roast prime rib and old-fashioned boiled beef.

SOY SAUCE

For all recipes using soy sauce
I recommend specifically the
natural flavor of Kikkoman soy
sauce which I prefer because its
mellowness blends with many
different kinds of food. Kikkoman
is an authentic Japanese soy
sauce, made of nutritious soybeans
and wheat, slowly fermented to
develop its full flavor.

GREEN ONION BUTTER

Cook in covered pan until clear
but not brown:
2 tablespoons onion, minced in
2 tablespoons butter
Whirl in blender 1 minute:
cooked onion
3 green onion tops, chopped fine
2 tablespoons water
dash herb salt*
Whip until light and fluffy:
1/2 pound butter (at room
temperature)
Add and whip until blended:
onion mixture
2 drops green coloring
This sauce is excellent on baked,
boiled or mashed potatoes; also
on steamed rice.

SWEET PEPPER BUTTER

Steam until soft then chop fine:
1 green pepper
Cut into very small bits:
1 pimiento
Whip until light and fluffy:
1/2 pound butter (at room
temperature)
Add:
1/2 teaspoon herb salt*
Fold green pepper and pimiento
into butter. This will keep in
the refrigerator for a long
time—except that it's so good
it never lasts long.

SAUCE ZOIA
WITH MUSHROOMS

Some years ago, Zoia Ross, and her
husband Will moved to Ojai.
Born in Russia, she worked for
the Red Cross in Turkey, and in
this country had helped Russian
immigrants to get settled. Her
culinary skill was unusual and she
gave me many wonderful Russian
recipes. She said a Russian
restaurant in New York City served
this sauce with kasha (buckwheat
groats). With any type of rice, this
makes an excellent luncheon dish.

It is also delicious served over
tournedos of beef, with scrambled
eggs or over sautéed fish. For
an unusual treat, try filling
Yorkshire puddings (page 89)
with this marvelous sauce for
a luncheon entree.

Braise until clear but not
too brown:
3 cups onion, sliced very thin in
1/4 pound butter
Add and cook 2 or 3 minutes:
1 pound mushrooms, sliced thin
Add and stir in:
1 tablespoon beef base (Bovril)
1/2 teaspoon meat herb blend*,
ground in
1/2 teaspoon herb salt*
Mix together and add, stirring
in well:
1/2 cup whole milk
1 cup béchamel sauce (page 24)
1-1/2 cups sour cream
1/2 teaspoon Kitchen Bouquet
(use no more—too bitter)
Reheat to serve but do not boil
as the sauce tends to curdle.

sauces

ITALIAN SAUCE

Cook until clear:
2 cups onions, chopped fine
4 cloves garlic, minced in
4 tablespoons olive oil
Add and boil slowly 15 minutes:
2 large green peppers, cut fine
4 bay leaves
(discard when cooked)
4 vegetable cubes
1 46-ounce can tomato juice

Pound in mortar and add:
1 teaspoon salt
1/2 teaspoon rosemary
1/2 teaspoon thyme
1 teaspoon oregano
1 teaspoon basil
When vegetables are tender, add
and simmer 30 minutes:
3 small cans tomato paste
This can be frozen and used as
needed. Just chop out desired
portion without defrosting the
entire amount. Or, freeze in
ice-cube trays; when frozen store
cubes in freezer bag and use
as needed.

SPANISH SAUCE

Cook in kettle until vegetables
are tender but not mushy:
4 cups onions, chopped coarse
3 cups celery, sliced
1 cup green peppers, cut coarse
1 cup mushrooms, sliced
(optional)
1 small can ripe olives, chopped
1 cup cooked tomatoes, mashed
2 vegetable cubes
1/2 tablespoon salt
1 bay leaf
(discard when cooked)
1 clove garlic, minced
1/2 teaspoon tomato herb
blend*
When vegetables are done, add
and simmer 15 minutes:
3 small cans tomato paste
1 7-ounce can pimientos,
chopped
This can be frozen and used
as needed.

You may notice as you read the soup recipes and the sauce recipes that there is very little mention of the stock pot. During years of cooking without meat, I had to learn how to make tasty and hearty sauces and soups without depending on meat broths as a flavoring foundation. (Why accept that only chicken or veal stock will make a rich cream soup?) With suitable herbs and spices one learns to enhance the natural flavor of whatever vegetable is used to make the soup or whatever ingredients are used to make the sauce. Without such knowledge the vegetarian diet would be bleak indeed!

Texture, so important in other dishes, is no less important to soup. Finely cut and lightly cooked vegetables, added to the soup for texture, will also impart extraordinary freshness, especially in soups made with a clear or semi-clear broth.

Cream soups do not need much thickening; some need none at all.

Selecting the best herb for a soup depends somewhat on whether it is a clear soup, a thick soup, a cream soup or a chilled soup. But the dominant flavor of the soup before herbs are added dictates which ones are to be used.

Fresh herbs are always best, but the dried ones are quite good also. They should be first ground in a mortar so that their flavors will marry with the flavor of the soup. Having large pieces of herbs floating in the soup is not recommended except for special things like fresh watercress.

Remember that cream soups should be delicately flavored, chicken a bit stronger, and beef or lamb can have a still stronger accent of herbs. Here are typical soup herb bouquets:

Cream soups: Equal parts parsley, basil, celery or lovage or marjoram; 1/2 part thyme; 1/4 part summer savory (a very strong herb).

Chicken-base soups: Equal parts chives, basil, marjoram, tarragon; 1/4 part sage, summer savory.

Beef-base soups: Equal parts summer savory, celery or lovage, parsley, basil, marjoram, thyme, chives.

soups

CHICKEN GUMBO SOUP

At various times I lived in
New Orleans where I acquired
a taste for gumbo and have
loved it ever since. Some people
do not like gumbo the first time
they taste it. But if you will
try it a few times, you will
probably learn to love it too.

You will need to get gumbo filé
for this soup, and be sure you
have the authentic New Orleans
variety which contains powdered
sassafras and a little thyme.
It can be ordered from the New
Orleans Importing Company,
New Orleans, Louisiana 70130, if
your market does not have it.
Chicken or turkey gizzards or
pieces of either can be used in
this soup. The gizzards make
a wonderful rich broth for
the soup.

Simmer covered, for 1/2 hour:
**3/4 pound chicken or turkey
gizzards**
2 cups water
Add, and simmer for
1-1/2 hours:
**5 pounds chicken or turkey
necks and backs**
4 cups water
(Add more water, if necessary,
as broth is cooking.)
Strain broth, allow to cool and
skim off fat. Remove skin and
bones from chicken; then chop
chicken meat and gizzards fine
and reserve. Combine and simmer
about 1/2 hour, or until
vegetables are tender:
2 cups of the chicken broth
3/4 cup celery, cut fine
1/2 cup onions, chopped fine
**2 tablespoons parsely,
chopped fine**
2 bay leaves
(very essential; discard
when cooked)
1/4 teaspoon salt
1/8 teaspoon paprika
1/2 tablespoon sugar
3 chicken cubes
1/8 teaspoon black pepper
**1/2 No. 303 can tomatoes,
mashed**

Add and cook until cornstarch
clears:
**1-1/4 tablespoons cornstarch
dissolved in a little water**
Now add, stirring the mixture
well, and skim if necessary:
**1 No. 303 can okra (or
2 cups fresh, cooked okra)**
4 cups water
**2 cups of the chicken broth
the reserved chopped chicken
or turkey**
1/2 cup cooked ham, minced
Add, stirring in quickly and
using wire whisk, for the powder
may get into little balls if not
quickly whisked into the liquid:
2 tablespoons gumbo filé
Heat again and skim off any fat
that comes to the top. Do not
boil, as the gumbo then becomes
slimy because of the okra.
Serves 6

MEXICAN CHICKEN SOUP

This is an easy soup to make, almost as simple as the barbequed chicken soup recipe just given. Actually, it is a variation of that recipe, although quite different in taste.

Prepare a rich chicken broth, by simmering for 1-1/2 hours:
**5 pounds chicken necks
and/or backs
4 cups water**

Drain, skim and reserve broth. Discard skin, take meat from bones, chop fine and reserve. Cook in pressure cooker without the cap, for 1 minute only, or steam in covered pan until vegetables are tender-crisp:
**1/4 cup water
1 chicken cube
1 small onion, minced
1/4 green pepper, minced
1 small stalk celery, minced
1/2 zucchini, minced
1 teaspoon soup herbs***
1 bay leaf
(discard when cooked)

Mix together:
**chicken broth, water added
if necessary, to make 4 cups
1-1/2 tablespoons cilantro, minced
3/4 tablespoon beef-stock
concentrate
1 tablespoon lemon juice
salt to taste
chopped chicken meat**
Heat to serving temperature and garnish with:
**1 avocado, cubed
pinch of cilantro (optional)**
Serves 6

soups

BARBEQUED CHICKEN SOUP

The first time Paul Newman and his wife Joanne Woodward came to the Ranch House we had this soup. He said, "I'll try it— but how can you barbeque a soup?" He liked it.

Most markets nowadays have electric barbeque machines in connection with their meat departments. Take a plastic container that has a cover and ask your butcher to reserve for you some of the broth that comes from the chicken as it is being barbequed. Ask him to save only the chicken drippings, not a mixture of sauces from other barbequed meats. If you bring home too much sauce, part of it can be frozen for future use. You will find that this sauce is very salty and rich; it must be diluted for your soup. Proceed little by little in mixing the sauce and the water until the mixture satisfies your taste requirements. You will need a quart of the mixture for this recipe.

soups

Cook in pressure cooker without cap for 1 minute, or steam in covered pan until vegetables are tender-crisp:
1/2 cup water
1 small onion, minced
1/4 green pepper, minced
1 small stalk celery, minced
1/2 zucchini, minced
1/2 teaspoon soup herb blend*
1 bay leaf
(discard when cooked)
1 tablespoon lemon juice

Add cooked vegetables to diluted barbeque sauce and heat to serving temperature.
Serves 4

AUTHENTIC
VIETNAMESE SOUP

This is another of the recipes given me by Mr. So, the Chinese gentleman from Viet Nam whose recipe which we call Beef Bali Hai is given in the section on meats. On the last night of my visit to Paris, he invited us for a special dinner which he prepared himself. It was another evening as delightful as the first one had been. I listened most sympathetically as he reminisced about his struggle to establish himself in Paris. His first restaurant, he told us, was just ten feet wide, with little tables along one wall, a tiny kitchen and a second floor of the same size. Students from the nearby Sorbonne flocked to the tiny restaurant for the delicious Vietnamese dishes he served. Here is the soup he gave us that night:

Prepare a rich broth, by simmering for 1-1/2 hours:
5 pounds chicken necks, backs, wings
4 cups water
Strain, skim and reserve broth and the meat from the chicken. Mix together:
1 cup cooked rice
1 cup flaked crab meat
1 teaspoon cilantro
1 teaspoon herb salt* or
1 chicken cube
salt to taste if cube is used
meat from chicken parts
4 cups chicken broth
(Add water to broth to make 4 cups if needed.) Heat to serving temperature and garnish with:
finely chopped fresh cilantro
Serves 6

33

soups

SOUP OF THE CASBAH

Although Charles Boyer denied saying, "Take me to the Casbah," I think he maght have said it if he had heard that in one of those little hole-in-the-wall restaurants they were serving this soup, sopped up with plenty of dark, hearty bread! But if you can't get away to this mysterious place, you can try it in less adventurous circumstances, right in your own home.

Braise in an open pan in 400° oven for about 30 minutes until meat is nicely browned, to get that dark-brown taste:
4 pounds lamb neck, cut into 4 pieces
Put browned lamb in pressure cooker with 4 cups of water and cook for 30 minutes at 15 pounds pressure or simmer in covered kettle for several hours. When done, remove meat from bones and chop fine. Allow broth to cool, skim off fat and add chopped meat. Now add and cook for 20 minutes at 15 pounds pressure, or until vegetables are tender in a covered kettle:

1 onion, chopped fine
2 stalks celery, chopped fine
1 green pepper, chopped fine
1 large carrot, chopped fine
1 clove garlic, chopped fine
1-1/4 cups lentils
1 bay leaf
(discard when cooked)
4 cups water
3 tablespoons beef base

Garnish with:
paper-thin slices of fresh lime
or a dollop of yogurt
Serves 6

OXTAIL WITH BARLEY

As I have mentioned elsewhere, my English-born grandmother lived with us when I was young. She was a superb cook and one of her specialities was soup. Here is one of her recipes using that wonderful grain, barley, which somehow seems to have gone out of fashion. This recipe may revive your interest in barley and put extra nourishment in the stomachs of those to whom you serve it. The English still make barley water, flavoring it with lemon, as a nourishing drink. It is even sold in stores as a soft drink. There are two things you must do today if you are to have this soup tomorrow.

Soak overnight:
1/2 cup barley, in
4 cups water
Cook in pressure cooker at 15 pounds for 30 minutes, or simmer in covered kettle for several hours:
2 oxtails
4 cups water
When cool, strain broth and skim off fat. Remove meat from bones, chop fine and return meat to broth. Refrigerate overnight. Next day, skim off fat. Cook soaked barley in pressure cooker at 15 pounds for 15 minutes, or simmer until tender in covered pot.
Cook for 10 minutes in pressure cooker without cap, or in covered kettle:

4 cups water
3/4 cup onions, minced
1 small carrot, minced
1 stalk celery, minced
2 cloves garlic, minced
1 bay leaf
(discard when cooked)
3 tablespoons beef extract, salty type
Add the cooked barley and the oxtail and broth. Return to stove and reheat gently for at least 20 minutes, being careful not to scorch as the barley settles to the bottom and, since it is a starch, tends to stick.
Serves 10
(Any leftover soup can be reheated or can be frozen satisfactorily.)

soups

WHITE FISH SOUP WITH DILL DUMPLINGS

Sometimes at the fish market you cannot find just the type of fish you are accustomed to buying. Here is a recipe which will take whatever kind of white fish you find on hand, just so it is fish that will flake, such as ocean bass.

Grind together:
4 sprigs each tarragon, borage, basil
or 1 teaspoon fish herb blend*
2 teaspoons herb salt*
Bring to boil in 12 cups water and cook for 5 minutes:
2 pounds white fish
4 vegetable cubes
ground herb mixture

To make dumpling dough, mix together thoroughly:
2 cups all-purpose flour, sifted
1/2 teaspoon salt
4 teaspoons Royal baking powder
(Do not use any other type, as the "double-acting" does not rise until acted on by oven heat.)
1 tablespoon fresh dill weed, chopped.
(Dry dill may be used but is not as good.)
Add and rub together by hand until mixture feels like coarse corn meal:
1/4 cup vegetable shortening
(You may wish to substitute butter for this, because it gives a better flavor. If so, use 3/8 cup of butter. The vegetable oil, however, makes a lighter dumpling.)
In a measuring cup, beat:
1 egg
Add:
milk to make 3/4 cup liquid
Have egg and milk mixture at room temperature. Make a hole in the dry mixture to the bottom of the mixing bowl, so that when egg mixture is added it will go to the bottom. Mix quickly, just enough to incorporate ingredients. Do not overmix. Using a spoon and rubber scraper, dip the spoon in the hot soup; then take a small amount of dough and with the scraper push it off into the boiling soup. Keep doing this quickly until the top of the kettle of soup is covered with dumplings. (They will quickly rise to the top as you drop them in.) Cover the kettle immediately and cook for a few minutes until the dumplings are done. They should be moist on the outside and soft but not doughy on the inside. Serve immediately. Garnish each bowl with:
a sprig of fresh dill
Serves 8

soups

WATERCRESS & SORREL SOUP

Wash thoroughly and remove all tough stems from spinach, French sorrel and watercress. Use only fresh herbs, dried ones will not do.
Simmer for 5 minutes in large, deep cooking pot; do not brown:
1/4 pound butter
1/2 leek, white part only, chopped fine
Add and boil for 10 minutes:
3 cups water
4 potatoes, peeled and quartered
Add and simmer gently for 45 minutes:
1/2 cup French sorrel, chopped
1 head lettuce, diced
1 cup spinach, chopped
1 tablespoon chervil, chopped
1 teaspoon marjoram, chopped
1/2 teaspoon basil, chopped
2 teaspoons salt
5 cups boiling water
When finished simmering, put the vegetables through the blender in several small batches so they will not blow out the

top of the blender because of the heat. With the last batch include and blend only slightly:
1/2 bunch fresh watercress, tops only
Reserve some sprigs of watercress for garnishing.
Reheat soup to serving temperature and garnish each bowl with:
sprig of watercress
sprinkle of paprika
Serves 8

37

soups

CURRIED MUSHROOM SOUP

This recipe was given to me originally by Torre Taggart when she was helping me with the cooking in the early days of the Ranch House. At that time we used canned mushroom soup but this recipe, which has been altered by changes and additions, calls for fresh mushrooms which are immeasurably better.

Make a massala by cooking slowly over low heat until clear:
4 tablespoons butter
1 onion, minced very fine
1 clove garlic, minced very fine
Add and mix well:
2 teaspoons curry powder
Simmer the massala for at least 5 to 10 minutes on very low heat; then add and blend in well:

8 ounces mushrooms, chopped fine
5 vegetable or chicken cubes
Cook about 5 minutes until mushrooms are done, then add and mix in well:
8 tablespoons flour
Add, cook and stir until thick:
8 cups milk
Stir in, mixing well:
2 tablespoons lemon juice
3 tablespoons apricot jam or currant jelly
1 tablespoon sherry
peel of 1/2 lemon, chopped very fine
Keep warm for about 30 minutes to blend flavors. Serve, garnished with:
very thin slices of lemon or lime
Serves 8

ONION-CHEDDAR SOUP

In a heavy pot, simmer until golden brown:
4 onions, sliced coarse in
6 tablespoons butter
Add:
4 cups hot water
Mix in a blender; then add to onions:
2 cups hot water
10 ounces aged Cheddar cheese, grated
Add to mixture:
1/2 cup Kikkoman soy sauce
Heat to serving temperature. Garnish with:
chopped pimientos
Serves 6-8
If there is any soup left over it makes an excellent base for other soups, or you can add leftovers such as rice or millet or even diced potatoes.

CHINESE PEAS

Prepare preceding recipe for
Onion-Cheddar Soup.
Wash and cut stems from:
**1 pound Chinese peas, lightly
cooked**

Be sure to select only small,
tender peas. The large ones may
have tough fibers at the sides.
When the broth is done, add the
peas, cover and cook only enough
to make them tender. They cook
quickly as you will discover if
you have not cooked them before.
Serve in individual ramekins.
Serves 4

You can make a delicious main
luncheon dish by increasing
the quantity of the broth and
adding cooked rice with the peas.
Serve in large soup bowls, along
with a melon salad.

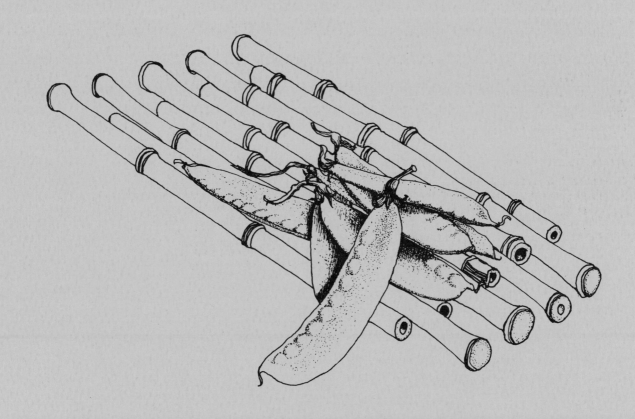

soups

CARNIVAL IN BASEL

In Basel, Switzerland, the pre-Lenten carnival is opened on the Monday preceding Ash Wednesday with a traditional pre-dawn breakfast of flour soup and cheese. At 4 a.m. there is a sounding of drums and flutes and the people come from all directions into town where the restaurants have prepared this special breakfast. At 5 a.m. they go to work so that they can quit at noon to begin their carnival festivities. There follows three days of drinking beer and dancing in the streets. I was served this soup by our Swiss friends Curt and Simone Walther. Here is her recipe. The cheese pie recipe is on page 57.

FLOUR SOUP

Brown in a large frying pan, stirring constantly, over low heat to prevent scorching:

1 cup white flour

When nicely brown add and mix well:

4 tablespoons butter

Add to desired thickness, stirring with a wire whisk:

8 cups chicken broth
pinch basil
pinch marjoram

Adjust flavor with:

salt to taste

Bring ingredients to a good boil and cook for about 5 minutes very slowly. Serve in large soup bowls with a good sprinkling of:

aged Emmentaler cheese, grated parsley, chopped fine

FRESH SALMON CHOWDER

Salmon collars are the neck portions of the fresh salmon that are cut off when the fish is cut into steaks. Ask your fish market to reserve these for you, or the small pieces left when the steaks are cut. Of course the steaks themselves can be used, if you can afford the extravagance. This is one of the finest dishes that can be made from fresh salmon.

Boil until just done,
don't overcook:
2 pounds salmon
1 cup water
Drain, skim and reserve liquid. Remove bones, skin and dark parts from fish. Fry until clear; do not brown:
1 small onion, chopped fine, in
2 tablespoons butter
Parboil for 5 minutes in enough water to cover:
2 cups potatoes, peeled and cut into 1/2-inch cubes
Drain and add potatoes and fish liquid to cooked onions.

Grind in mortar:
1 teaspoon salt
1 teaspoon herb salt*
1/8 teaspoon fish herbs blend*
1/8 teaspoon white pepper
Add herb mixture to potato and onion mixture, cook for 5 minutes, cover and simmer about 10 minutes; then add:
1 cup coffee cream
1 cup scalded milk
5 soda crackers, soaked in
a little of the milk
2 tablespoons butter
the cooked salmon
Do not boil, but serve very hot. Too much heating may curdle the soup. If this happens, drain off liquid and put it through blender; then mix with solids and reheat.
Serves 6

CLAM CHOWDER, NEW ENGLAND STYLE

Mix together in a saucepan:
3 tablespoons butter
5 tablespoons flour
Add and cook until thickened:
4 cups milk
1 13-ounce can evaporated milk
1 milk can of water

Remove rind, cut into small cubes and fry until crisp but not too brown:
1 ounce salt pork
Remove pork from fat and reserve. Add to pork fat and cook until clear:
1 small onion, chopped fine
Peel, dice and cook in 1/2 cup water until done but not mushy:
2 small potatoes
Mix all ingredients together and add as seasoning:
1-1/2 teaspoons herb salt*
pinch caraway seeds
1 tablespoon sherry
Adjust seasoning with:
salt to taste (about
1-1/2 teaspoons)
dash white pepper
Add and stir in:
1-1/2 pints minced clams
and juice
Heat in double boiler to serving temperature, no hotter, as it tends to curdle after clams have been added.
Garnish with:
chopped parsley
paprika
Serves 8

soups

TOMATO SOUP WITH CLOVEN HOOF

Boil for about 10 minutes:
8 medium-sized tomatoes, unpeeled, cut up
2 cups water
While still hot, put into muslin cloth and hang to drain as you would in making jelly. Add to drained juice:
1 teaspoon sugar for each cup of juice
powdered cloves
only as much as can be picked up on the point of a paring knife. Use caution! Too much will overpower the tomato flavor. You can always add more, but you can't take it out once it is in.
salt to taste
red coloring, 1 drop
Subtleness is the secret of this wonderful soup. If you get the proper proportions it will delight you. Tomatoes vary in flavor so you must be gentle with the cloves each time you make it, bringing all of your gourmet artistry to bear in concocting this seemingly simple recipe. It should be a clear, bright broth, not sharp, perfectly blended. For interest, add:
alphabet noodles, a few to each serving
or, as the Japanese do with their soups, add to each serving:
1 thin slice of fresh mushroom
a tiny slice of green pepper
the thinnest slice of celery
Serve hot or chilled.
Serves 4

FORDHOOK LIMA BEAN & HAM SOUP

Soak overnight:
1 cup large dry limas, in
6 cups water
Next day, using soaking water, cook beans slowly in covered pot until done, or at 15 pounds pressure for 15 minutes in pressure cooker, with:
1 pound ham shank
When done, discard fat and ham bone, chop ham fine and reserve it. Skim fat from liquid, put beans and liquid through blender, then add chopped ham.
Cook in covered pan for 10 minutes, or in pressure cooker for 1 minute at 15 pounds pressure:
1 cup water
1 clove garlic, minced
1 large onion, minced
1 stalk celery, minced
1 small green pepper, minced
2-1/4 teaspoons soup herb blend*
1-1/4 teaspoons herb salt*
6 soup cubes, chicken or vegetable
Add vegetables to broth, reheat to serving temperature. For an unusual garnish, make small balls of:
cream cheese
Roll cheeseballs in:
chopped parsley
Drop into each bowl of hot soup.
Serves 6

BELGIAN BEEF SOUP

Brown well in heavy skillet:
**1-1/2 pounds beef cross ribs,
cut in 4-inch pieces**
(Add no fat; there is
enough on the meat.)
Add to meat and cook until done:
**4 cups water
1 small onion, minced
1 bay leaf**
(discard when cooked)
**1-1/2 teaspoons soup herb blend*
1-1/2 teaspoons herb salt**
Cool, lift out meat, discard
bones and chop meat fine. Skim
broth well (or better,
refrigerate overnight and take
off fat).
Mix together and cook for
10 minutes, or in pressure
cooker at 15 pounds for 1 minute:

**1/2 onion, sliced very thin
1 small stalk celery, sliced thin
2 fresh string beans, sliced thin
1/2 green pepper, chopped fine
1 carrot, chopped fine
2 tablespoons lemon juice
2 cups water
6 beef soup cubes
broth from cross ribs**
When done, add:
chopped beef
If a heavier soup is desired,
fine noodles may be boiled
separately and added.
Serves 6

MULLIGATAWNEY

This is an East Indian curried
soup and a quite unusual,
flavorful combination of
ingredients.

Fry slowly for at least 5 minutes,
so it will brown without burning:
**1 cup carrots, chopped fine
1 cup green peppers, cut fine
1 cup tart green apples,
cut fine
1 cup onion, chopped fine in
4 tablespoons butter**
(clarified butter called ghee
is best)

Add and continue to cook slowly
until flour browns:
2 teaspoons flour
Mix together, add and boil
for about 2 minutes:
**8 cups chicken or beef broth
1-1/2 teaspoons curry powder
1 teaspoon salt
2 teaspoons chicken or beef base
1 cup yogurt, stirred well
1/4 teaspoon cardamon seed,
powdered
2 tablespoons tomato paste
2 teaspoons sugar
2-1/2 teaspoons lemon juice**
Add to finished soup:
1 cup cooked rice
Garnish with:
**a sprinkling of fresh, finely
grated coconut
or a paper-thin slice of lemon**
Serves 8

salads

"Let onion atoms lurk within
the bowl
And, half suspected,
animate the whole."

—Lady Holland

ENGLISH SALAD

This is a popular salad in England. It is easy to make and can be varied according to taste and leftover vegetables.
Mix together:
1 cup cooked carrots, diced
1 cup cauliflower, cut in
small pieces
2 green onions, tops only,
minced
1/4 teaspoon salt
1/2 cup mayonnaise, mixed with
1 teaspoon lemon juice
or vinegar
Arrange in bowl lined with:
lettuce leaves
Garnish with:
strips of pimiento
Serves 4

GREEN BEAN & ONION SALAD

Cook until done but not mushy, then drain and chill in refrigerator:
1 pound slender green beans
(The wide, coarse beans are too tough for this salad.)
Peel and slice very thin:
2 large Spanish onions

Prepare a marinade, having all ingredients at room temperature:
1/2 cup lemon juice
1/2 cup wine vinegar
1/4 teaspoon each tarragon, basil, marjoram, thyme
or 1 teaspoon salad herb blend*
1-1/2 teaspoons herb salt*
Add and mix well:
1 cup olive oil
Put 2/3 of the marinade over chilled and drained green beans and 1/3 of it over the sliced onions. Let both stand 15 minutes, then drain.
Line salad plates with:
lettuce leaves
Arrange green beans on the lettuce, put a small mound of onion slices on them and garnish with:
thin strips of pimiento
a few capers
Chill well on the plates before serving.
Serves 6

RAW SPINACH WITH SHERRY DRESSING

For this salad, use only the small leaves, no large ones or stems. Wash carefully, then dry before using and chill thoroughly:
spinach leaves to serve 4
Hardboil and slice:
2 eggs
Cook until crisp:
4 slices bacon

To make dressing mix together with wire whip:
1/3 cup sherry
1/4 cup olive oil
3 tablespoons vinegar
1 teaspoon lime juice
1/2 teaspoon herb salt*
black pepper, 2 turns of pepper mill
small pinch curry powder

Line salad plates with:
bronze lettuce leaves
Toss chilled spinach with sherry dressing and pile on lettuce leaves; top each portion with egg slices and a crumbled strip of bacon.
Garnish with:
strips of pimiento
Serve ice cold.

salads

COMBINATION ASPIC SALAD

The main ingredients of this salad come from the can. It is a good thing to know about for emergency situations; a small can of each in the refrigerator and you're ready for anything:
tomato aspic
beet aspic
asparagus spears
Cut 1/2-inch thick rounds of the tomato and beet aspic and lay 1 of each on:
lettuce leaf
Lay on top of the aspic rounds:
1 or 2 asparagus spears
Add:
sour cream dressing (page 52)
Garnish with:
strip of pimiento
Serves 8, or more

CABBAGE COMBINATION

Steam for 1 minute only, then drain and chill:
1/2 head of cabbage cut into 1/2-inch cubes
When cabbage has chilled, mix it with:
2 cups celery, sliced thin
2 cups unpeeled apples, cut in 1/2-inch cubes
1 cup broken pecans
To make dressing, mix in blender:
1/2 pint sour cream
3 ounces Philadelphia cream cheese
1/2 teaspoon poppy seeds
dash turmeric
1/2 teaspoon salt
dash onion salt to taste
Combine cabbage mixture and dressing. For each serving, line salad plate with:
lettuce leaf
With ice-cream scoop, put a mound of salad on the lettuce. Garnish generously with:
minced parsley
Pass a bowl of:
French dressing
for those who want a variation in flavor.
Serves 8, or more

FOOD FADDIST SALAD

Toss together lightly:
1 bunch watercress, chopped coarse
1 cup bean sprouts
1/2 cup celery leaves
1 cup alfalfa sprouts
1 cup sprouted wheat (not too old, or leaves will be tough)

To make dressing, mix in blender:
1/2 cup soy oil
1/4 cup lemon juice
1/2 teaspoon sea salt (available at health food stores)
1/2 cup parsley tops
1/4 teaspoon tarragon
1/4 teaspoon marjoram
4 mint leaves

Toss salad and dressing together. Line salad plates with:
lettuce leaves
Mound salad on lettuce and top with:
avocado slices
Serves 8

BIG STINKY SALAD

Here's something great to serve with barbequed steaks or a beef roast in place of the usual tossed green salad. Once you bring yourself to concocting the Big Stinky, you'll repeat it many times. It's best when broccoli and the other vegetables are first in season, with small and tender stalks.

Put into the freezer so that it will be frozen when you are ready to use it:
1/4 pound Danish blue cheese
For each 4 servings steam only until tender, then drain and chill:
2 large heads broccoli, cut up
1 small head cauliflower, cut up
4 brussel sprouts
8 asparagus spears

To make dressing, mix together:
1/2 pint sour cream
1/4 cup French capers
1 teaspoon salad herb blend*
1/2 teaspoon onion salt
1/4 teaspoon garlic salt
For each serving line salad plate with:
lettuce leaf

Arrange chilled vegetables on lettuce. Spoon over them some of the dressing in a way to enhance the arrangement, not cover it up. With a sharp knife shave off a generous amount of the frozen blue cheese onto each portion. The freezing makes it easy to handle this sticky cheese. Garnish generously with:
minced parsley
The parsley is the only garnish needed as the salad is supposed to be green and greenish white in color.

RICE-AND-SUCH SALAD

Cook and chill:
1 cup white rice
Mix rice together with:
1/2 teaspoon nutmeg
1/2 cup chopped almonds
1/2 cup pine nuts (pignolias)
1/2 cup raisins
Add, just enough to hold mixture together:
mayonnaise
Mold mixture into small balls, 3 to a serving. Lay rice balls on:
lettuce leaf
Add in an attractive arrangement:
3 slices avocado
Serve with a bowl of:
Samoa sour cream dressing
(page 53)

salads

EXQUISITE FRUIT SALAD

Arrange on lettuce leaf:
avocado slices
grapefruit sections
Put in blender and blend until
smooth:
1 cup mayonnaise
1/2 cup sour cream
1/4 cup powdered sugar
2 leaves mint
4 orange blossoms (optional)
1/2 cup strawberries
Spoon the dressing over the fruit
in dabs, then sprinkle lightly
with:
raw pignolia nuts
The color of this dressing will
delight you. It can be used on
many other combinations, such as
lime jello with pineapple cubes
and nuts.
Dressing serves 8

MELON FIESTA SALAD

Make this salad when all the
melons are at the peak of their
season. Get as many varieties as
you can, and remember, ripeness
is the secret of success with
this salad.
watermelon, ruby ripe, cut in
1-inch thick triangular slices
cantaloupe, cut in strips
Persian, cut in strips
honeydew, cut in strips
casaba, cut in strips
Crenshaw, cut in strips
Chill the sliced melons in a big
bowl in the refrigerator for at
least 4 hours before serving, for
they must be ice cold when served.

Line the fanciest platter you own
with:
bronze lettuce leaves
Around the platter arrange
portions of:
cottage cheese
using a small ice-cream scoop. Lay
1 each of the melon slices around
each mound in an attractive design
without covering the cheese.
Dribble over each mound of cheese,
leaving some of it exposed for
color:
grenadine sour cream dressing
(page 52)
Sprinkle on the dressing:
freshly grated coconut
Place on each mound:
1 red cherry
1 green cherry
This is an elegant dish for a
luncheon party, served with bread
or hot rolls and iced tea.

salads

FRESH FRUIT WITH POMEGRANATE DRESSING

Line salad plate with:
bronze lettuce leaf
Arrange on lettuce:
fresh fruit slices
Whip in mixer at high speed:
1/2 pint sour cream
4 ounces Philadelphia cream cheese
1/4 cup pomegranate sauce (recipe follows)
or 1/4 cup grenadine
For texture, sprinkle on:
fresh coconut
pomegranate seeds (optional)
Dressing serves 8

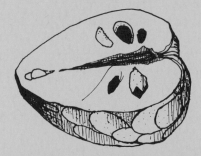

POMEGRANATE SAUCE

Select the darkest colored, ripest fruit you can find. Try not to use the light pink pomegranates as their flavor is not so deep and rich as that of the fully matured ones.
Cut in half and juice as you would an orange:
pomegranates, as many as you wish
When juicing the pomegranates, use side pressure against the juicer cone to extract all the juice. And watch out, for juice may fly in all directions!
Reserve some of the seeds to use as a garnish; they are fine for adding interest and color.
Get at the market one of the prepared packages of:
pectin for jelly making
Follow the instructions on the package as you would for making berry jelly. The jelly may be a bit thick; you can stir or put it in the blender to thin it down if you wish.
This sauce is excellent served over ice cream or other desserts and is useful in salad dressings, as called for in this chapter.

FRESH FRUIT WITH CARDAMON SAUCE

If you are not familiar with this spice, here is a sauce recipe that will demonstrate its wonderful flavor. On fresh fruit, it will offer a happy taste experience.
Simmer over low heat for 2 minutes to blend flavors:
1/2 cup water
1/2 cup orange blossom honey
1/4 teaspoon cardamon seed, powdered
6 large mint leaves, chopped (dried mint will not do)
1/4 teaspoon salt
Cool to room temperature, then add and stir in well:
1/2 cup good port wine
1/8 cup Benedictine
Peel and slice enough for 8 servings:
melon, all kinds
avocado
apple
oranges
Arrange fruit attractively on salad plates lined with:
red lettuce leaves
Garnish plates of fruit with:
parsley
pitted black cherries

JAVANESE SALAD

Mix together:
1/2 teaspoon cream of tartar
2 cups cold water
Peel, then dip immediately into cream of tartar solution:
4 bananas
This will keep the bananas from turning dark. Drain them well for at least 30 minutes.
Chop fine and spread on foil or a plate:
1 cup peanuts or blanched almonds
Roll the bananas in the nuts. The bananas will be very sticky and can be nicely coated with the nuts.
Prepare:
1 avocado, peeled and sliced
1 papaya, peeled and sliced
1 mango, peeled and sliced (optional)
pineapple slices, fresh or canned

Mix together:
1 cup mayonnaise
1/2 cup lime marmalade
2 tablespoons creme de menthe or less, according to taste
Line 4 salad plates with:
lettuce
Lay the coated banana on the lettuce leaf, arrange the sliced fruit around it in an attractive pattern, and spoon on some of the dressing. In Java, you would put fresh flowers on the table and scatter a few of their petals on each salad plate.

salads

RANCH HOUSE SALAD DRESSING

Mix well together:
1 cup wine vinegar
1/2 teaspoon dry mustard
1/2 teaspoon fresh-ground black pepper
Grind together and mix in:
4 sprigs basil
4 sprigs marjoram
2 sprigs tarragon
2 sprigs lemon thyme
2 sprigs rosemary
1 teaspoon herb salt*
(Use only fresh herbs, dry will not do.)
Add and mix in:
2 cups olive oil
Do not refrigerate.

SOUR CREAM DRESSING
(For vegetable and aspic salads)

Put into mixer and whip thoroughly:
1 pint sour cream
1/2 cup mayonnaise
1 teaspoon onion salt
1/2 teaspoon garlic salt
1/2 teaspoon salad herbs*
2 ounces Philadelphia cream cheese

GRENADINE SOUR CREAM DRESSING
(For fruit salads)

Put in mixer and whip until well blended:
1 pint sour cream (sour whipping cream is best)
2/3 cup powdered sugar
2 tablespoons grenadine
2 ounces Philadelphia cream cheese
1/4 cup mayonnaise (optional)

SESAME SEED DRESSING

A product available in specialty food shops is ground-up sesame seeds, sometimes called tahini. Like peanut butter, oil comes to the top and it has to be mixed before using. It is often eaten as a spread on dark bread, and it makes a delicious salad dressing. Mix together:

sesame seed butter, thinned with a very small amount of boiling water
lemon juice to taste
To give it a salty flavor you may add:
Kikkoman soy sauce to taste

SAMOA SALAD DRESSING

This delicious dressing is good on fresh fruit salads or desserts. You will need ginger marmalade that is made without lemon juice. There is a brand that comes from Ledbury, England, named after the town.

Put in mixer and whip until smooth:
1/2 pint sour cream
1/4 cup ginger marmalade (without lemon juice)
pinch of curry powder
For texture, sprinkle on:
raw, unsalted pignolia nuts
As a variation, instead of the curry powder add:
2 leaves pennyroyal, chopped
More marmalade may be used for stronger flavor, if desired.

PEANUT BUTTER DRESSING

Whip in mixer:
1/4 cup peanut butter
1 cup mayonnaise
1/3 cup honey
3/4 cup coffee cream
1 tablespoon sauterne
1-1/2 tablespoons lemon juice
4 ounces Philadelphia cream cheese
pinch of salt
If too thick, thin with cream.

salads

VARIATIONS ON THE TOSSED GREEN SALAD

Something new can be added to the old standby, for taste and visual pleasure. When using leaves from the flower plants, wash them carefully and add them, dry, to the lettuce. Judge the amount according to your taste, for unusual flavor combinations.
Rose petals If you have old-fashioned roses in your garden, gather a few fresh petals and scatter them over the salad just as you serve it. If the roses are of the right type, the fragrance, taste and texture will amaze you.

Pot marigold (Calundula) Sprinkle on a few petals. They'll add lots of color, and a unique taste.
English violet Pick the young plant leaves, mix them with the lettuce.
Nasturtium Use the young plant leaves, mix them with the lettuce.
Jicama A fine vegetable that comes from Mexico and is available in most markets. Peel off the thick skin, revealing the wonderfully textured meat. Slice thin, chill until very cold and top the salad with it. Its delicious sweet flavor will blend perfectly with the dressing.

cheese

I am not an authority on cheese and only speak from my experience with it. Of course, cheese varies with the country or area producing it. Some cheeses are so perishable thay cannot be shipped from their place of origin. There are myriad varieties, domestic and foreign. Each cook must choose favorites, looking for qualities of flavor and texture within each class. On the Swiss Independence Day I attended a dinner that had as its feature 100 varieties of cheese that had been sent from all over Europe. What a feast! New, green cheese will not melt but turns into a sort of soft, stringy gum. Aging somehow affects the cheese so that it will melt. As much as a year is required to age good cheese properly. To make green cheese more soluble, and perhaps to dilute the more expensive aged cheese, it is "processed" by the addition of gums, water, powdered milk, etc.; it lacks the quality and rich flavor of aged cheese. The cheese used in Welsh rarebit and in fondues should always be aged. A simple way to tell whether or not cheese is aged is to break it. Aged cheese will crumble easily; green cheese will not.

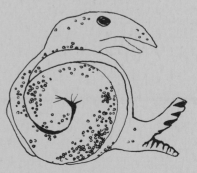

cheese

FONDUE GRUYÈRE

Whenever we visit Switzerland we go to the Chateau Gruyère where that famous cheese was first made. In the little village they make the traditional fondue which is supposed to have originated there, and they taught me how to make it. Here is the original recipe; there are variations but this is how it was prepared and served to us.
Heat in a pottery fondue dish which has been rubbed with garlic clove:

1-1/2 cups dry white wine
Grate and mix together:
1/2 pound aged Gruyère cheese
1/2 pound aged Emmentaler cheese
Add the grated cheese to the heated wine and stir until it begins to dissolve. As you stir it may seem to be making a sticky ball. Do not despair! All will be well. Sieve and stir in, to bring the cheese and wine together to a good smooth consistency:

3 tablespoons potato starch (no other starch will work) do not first dissolve in water

Keep stirring and add:
2 or 3 tablespoons Kirsch (cherry brandy, also called Kirschwasser)
dash nutmeg (optional)
When the mixture is smooth and begins to thicken slightly, take the casserole to the table and place over a small alcohol stove. At Gruyère each guest is provided with a long two-tined fork with a wooden handle. A large wooden bowl, placed within everybody's reach, is filled with chunks of sourdough or French bread. With your fork spear a piece of bread and dip it into the fondue, turning it to catch the drip as you lift it out. Anyone who drops a piece of bread into the fondue is kissed by the girl next to him. At the last there forms on the bottom of the casserole a browned crust which everyone fights for.
Serves 6

56

FRIED CHEESE BALLS

Mix together:
2 cups grated Cheddar cheese
1 cup cottage cheese
1 egg, beaten
1 cup bread crumbs
1/4 teaspoon herb salt*
1/2 teaspoon savory herb blend*
Form the mixture into balls and
roll them in bread crumbs. Drop
into hot oil—375°, and brown.
Serve with a good sprinkling of:
parsley, minced

To make an appetizing luncheon
dish, dribble over the cheeseballs:
béchamel sauce (page 24)
Garnish with the parsley and
serve with green beans and
yellow squash mixed with
fresh peas.
Serves 4 - 6

CHEESE PIE

Line a shallow, round 9-inch
pan with:
rich pastry crust
Crimp edges so they will hold up
making it easy to remove the
pieces when baked.
Mix together the following
ingredients:
**1-1/2 cups milk (or part cream
for extra richness)**
3 eggs, beaten
1/2 teaspoon salt
1/4 teaspoon white pepper
Line pastry shell with:
**aged Emmentaler cheese,
sliced then**
Pour in egg and milk mixture.
Bake at 350° for about
40 minutes until the custard is
set. Many variations of this pie
have been invented but the
original is this very simple and
very good quiche from Alsace
Lorraine. Often these pies are
made in smaller sizes, about
3 to 4 inches. But the large ones
are better because they don't
dry out so much in the baking.

FRIED CHEESE SQUARES

Cut into 1-inch cubes:
1 pound Monterey jack cheese
Dip cheese squares into:
flour
then into:
1 egg, beaten with
1 teaspoon water
then into:
bread crumbs
Drop into hot oil, 375° until
lightly browned. If cooked too
long the cheese will become
stringy. If the breading is thick
enough, they will be crisp on the
outside, an interesting contrast
to the inside softness. Don't be
afraid to experiment. They make
an excellent luncheon entree.
Serves 4

cheese

QUICHE LORRAINE

This is the original Swiss recipe.

Line glass pie pan with:
rich pie crust (make it thin)
Fry until very crisp, then drain
on paper towel:
8 slices bacon, cut thick
Put in blender:
4 eggs
1 tablespoon flour
1/2 teaspoon salt
**2 cups cream (a little heavier
than coffee cream)**
dash nutmeg
**1/2 teaspoon Worcestershire
sauce**
dash cognac (optional)
Blend only until mixed. Do not
overblend or custard will not
set right.
Crumble bacon slices in pie
crust; cover with thin slices of:
aged Swiss cheese
Add egg mixture and bake at 350°
until custard sets.
Serves 6

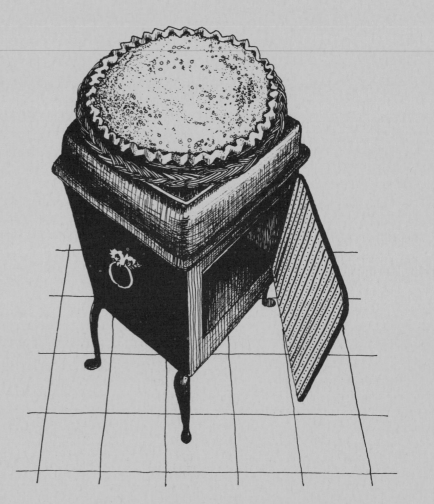

Traditionally cooks use a few basic herbs in egg dishes.

A primary one is tarragon which blends so well with basil and marjoram that it is always safe to add these three in equal proportions to any egg dish. Thyme and summer savory may be added, though only with great discretion, else their stronger flavors will dominate the dish and spoil it. Be equally sparing with strong herbs like rosemary and sage. When you do use the stronger herbs, start with about 1/8 as much as you would use of the traditional tarragon-basil-marjoram bouquet.

An excellent herb which I do not find on the grocer's shelf but which can be so easily grown (year around in moderate climates), is costmary. This fine herb with its delicate mint flavor is a tasty addition to an egg dish. It is different from other mint herbs because it is not so penetrating, much more subtle. Try it; you will be delighted with it. Other common herbs—celery, onion and capsicum (green pepper)—augment the flavor when used with eggs. Lovage and chervil are also excellent in combination, in about the same proportions as the traditional three

Eggs are a multipurpose food, used on their own or in combinations or to aid in the structure of some more complicated dish. Thus one has to know in what way they are going to be used in order to understand the kind of flavoring needed. If cooked alone in various ways, a little sprinkling of a delicate herb mixture and salt ground together—a mere suggestion of an herb blend—is excellent. Combined with other things such as vegetables or mushrooms, the traditional bouquet is excellent. If they lose their identity as they bind things together in other dishes, the herbs used will be those that complement the main ingredients.

eggs

CURRIED, STUFFED EGGS

Boil gently for 10 minutes, starting in cold water; do not let eggs roll in the boiling water:
12 eggs
Cool eggs, dipping them in cold water to make them easy to handle, peel off the shells and cut the eggs across. Gently remove the yolks without damaging the whites. Reserve whites and yolks.
Fry gently until onions are clear:
1 clove garlic, minced
1 small onion, minced in
2 tablespoons butter
Add and continue to cook for 5 minutes over low heat:
2 tablespoons curry powder
few drops lemon juice

Mash egg yolks and mix into the curry; then press this mixture into the egg-white halves. Put the filled halves together and secure them with toothpicks; lay them in a casserole.
Heat together:
4 tablespoons butter
4 tablespoons flour
Add and cook, stirring constantly with wire whisk until thick:
2 cups milk
1/2 cup coffee cream
1 bay leaf
(discard when cooked)
1/2 teaspoon herb salt* or regular salt
1 tablespoon sherry
Pour sauce over eggs in casserole, reheat to serving temperature and serve, accompanied by rice. Remove toothpicks gently as eggs are spooned out on plate, so that the eggs will not come apart.
Serves 6 - 8

OMELETTE CHANTILLY

Cook until done but not mushy:
2 onions, sliced thin
2 shallots, minced (optional) in
2 tablespoons butter
Add and stir in well:
6 tablespoons coffee cream
2 tablespoons white flour
2 teaspoons egg herb blend*
Let cool so that when egg yolks are added they will not thicken.
Beat until lemon colored:
8 egg yolks
1/4 teaspoon salt
Beat until stiff but not dry:
8 egg whites
1/4 teaspoon salt
Fold into the egg whites:
2 teaspoons fresh dill weed, chopped
1/2 cup fresh parsley, minced

Dry dill may be substituted but the flavor is much weaker. Mix the egg yolks with the onion mixture and then fold in the beaten whites, mixing very little. There should be large chunks of the whites left unmixed, for the required texture of the dish. Turn into heavily buttered casserole and bake at 400° for about 20 minutes or until a knife inserted comes out clean. Serve immediately. There should be parts of the egg white showing with flecks of the dill. This, and the distinctive dill flavor give the omelette its character.
Serves 6

vegetables

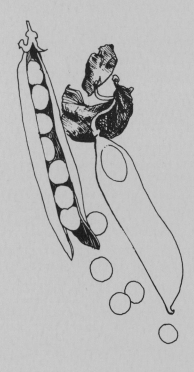

Vegetables more than 24 hours old, not refrigerated or preserved in some manner, have lost 90 percent of their food value say authorities on nutrition. The natural sugar content of the vegetable is what gives it its delicious flavor and when its freshness is lost, this sugar turns to starch. So, when freshness is lost practically all is lost, both flavor and nutrition.

The best way to preserve the precious sugar in cooked vegetables is to see that the cooking time is short, so that it does not bleed out into the water or get driven off in the steam along with the volatile oils. For this reason, I suggest pressure cooking for most vegetables; also, the quick pressure cooking preserves the natural color of the vegetable. Often the pressure cooker can be used without the cap, as there is still more pressure than there would be in a kettle with the closest-fitting lid. Some vegetables take only a half minute to cook in the pressure cooker so it is a good idea to use a timer if you have one. When the pressure cap is used the cooker has to be cooled immediately under the cold water tap to prevent overcooking.

In China and Japan they know the delight of quickly cooked, crisp vegetables which they cook in a wok, a wonderful cooking gadget. Most gourmet shops have them. As far as I am able to discover, vegetables are cooked best, not in Europe but in America—especially in California. In France, I have experienced the horror of gray, limp haricots verts with no sauce, not even butter; it is almost sacrilege thus to ruin these small, tender beans.

PAN-COOKED VEGETABLES

For those who for one reason or another do not want to use a pressure cooker, here is an easy and uncomplicated way to prepare many vegetables. Use a large frying pan that can be tightly covered. Electric fry pans are excellent for this. Coat the vegetables with your favorite oil or melted butter, usually 2 to 4 tablespoons. Cook over low heat, stirring frequently and gently so that the vegetables do not stick. Most will provide their own juice. If some like cabbage are a little dry, add water sparingly, a tablespoon at a time. Keep the pan covered as much as possible.

The vegetables should be chopped or sliced thin. Any combination that appeals to you can be cooked together, but always start with an onion. Think of all the new and exotic flavor blends you can discover.

Further interest and flavor may be achieved by adding, singly or in combination, light seasonings such as ground turmeric or ground coriander, usually about 1/4 teaspoon; 1/2 teaspoon fresh grated ginger, or a few mustard seeds. If you use spices, add them to the oil or butter and cook slowly for a couple of minutes before adding the onion and sliced vegetables, so that the flavors will blend.

Vegetables cooked this way can be served with steamed rice, plain or with herbs or nuts added. A topping of plain yogurt is excellent.

SUGGESTION FOR VEGETABLE VARIETY

As a change to give variety to cooked vegetables, put a light layer of cottage cheese over them and heat covered long enough for the cheese to get warm. For the vegetarian, this accompanied by rice topped with fresh yogurt provides adequate protein and good variation in flavors and textures.

vegetables

ZUCCHINI FRITTATI

To make a batter, separate:
4 eggs
Add to yolks and to whites:
1/2 teaspoon salt to each
(This will thicken the eggs and make the batter hold up.)
Grind together in mortar:
1/2 teaspoon dry basil
1/2 teaspoon dry marjoram
1/2 teaspoon dry oregano
1/2 teaspoon herb salt*
Mix ground herbs into:
4 tablespoons sifted flour
Beat egg yolks first until they are lemon colored and thick. Beat the whites until they are stiff but not dry. Gently fold yolks into whites and then fold in the flour mixture. Do this very gently, using a wire whip.

Add and gently fold in:
2 cups zucchini, cut in 1/4-inch slices and lightly salted
Heat in skillet:
1/2 cup peanut oil

Peanut oil will not burn or smoke as quickly as other oils and has a wonderful fragrance of its own to add to the food. Drop a large spoonful of the batter into the hot oil. Each cake should be about 3 inches across when done to make the frittati as flat as possible. Fry until nicely brown, turn and brown the other side. Serve cakes very hot with the following sauce poured over them.

Cook until soft but not mushy:
2 onions, sliced thin
6 tablespoons olive oil
Grind in mortar:
4 sprigs oregano
4 sprigs basil
4 sprigs thyme
1 sprig rosemary
1/2 teaspoon herb salt*
Peel and squeeze seeds from:
2 large tomatoes
Put tomatoes through coarse sieve to remove excess pulp.
Add:
2 vegetable cubes
the ground herb mixture
Add tomato and herb mixture to onions and cook for 5 minutes.
Add and cook until thickened:
2 cups water
3 tablespoons cornstarch
dissolved in a little of the water
Serves 8

vegetables

COLLARD GREENS

You will often find these greens in your supermarket. If you don't, mustard greens will make a good substitute. Here is how they're served in New Orleans.

Wash carefully, taking off any tough stems, put into a kettle and press down a little:
1/2 teaspoon marjoram
2 bunches greens
Cube and brown lightly:
4x4-inch piece of fat salt pork
Put the browned pork cubes on top of the greens and pour the fat over them. This gives the real Southern flavor. Add enough water to make about 1 inch in the bottom of the pot, and cook, covered, until done. Serve with corn bread over which the "pot liquor" has been poured.
Serves 8

CALIFORNIA BUTTERED BEETS

Cut off tops leaving about 1 inch of stems, scrub but do not peel:
10 beets (about 1-1/2 pounds)

Cook beets in pressure cooker with 2 cups water for 15 minutes at 15 pounds pressure or in covered pan until tender. Cool in running water and skins will slip off easily.
Slice the skinned beets and bring to boil in:
1 cup water
Drain and reserve beet juice.

Mix together:
1/4 cup fresh orange juice
1/4 cup honey
2 tablespoons cider vinegar
juice from cooked beets
1 tablespoon grated orange rind
1/4 tablespoon powdered cardamon
2 tablespoons cornstarch
Cook until slightly thickened, stirring with wire whip to prevent lumping.
Pour sauce over sliced beets and add:
2 tablespoons butter
Heat and maintain at serving temperature, allowing to marinate for at least 1 hour.
Serves 8

BEETS JAMAICA

Cut tops and tails from:
4 very large beets
Scrub beets and put them unpeeled through gricer, using medium cone. Cook in pressure cooker for 10 minutes at 15 pounds pressure with:
1/4 cup water
If you do not have a gricer, put them in a pot with enough water to cover and boil until tender. Drain the water and slip off the skins. Slice very thin. Blend together and stir until smooth:
3/4 teaspoon ground ginger (or 2 tablespoons freshly grated ginger)
1/2 cup sugar
1-1/2 tablespoons cornstarch
1/2 cup cider vinegar
Cook 5 minutes, stirring constantly to prevent sticking. Add and simmer gently for 10 minutes to blend flavors, stirring occasionally:
the cooked beets
4 tablespoons butter
Serve piping hot, garnished with plenty of:
parsley, finely chopped
Serves 6

HOLIDAY CAULIFLOWER

Wash, trim and steam whole in
covered kettle in 1 inch
of water, until just done:
1 head cauliflower
Make bread crumbs by running
through blender or crushing with
rolling pin:
3 slices stale white bread
Melt:
1/4 pound butter
Add:
1/2 teaspoon herb salt*
**1/2 teaspoon curry powder,
mixed with
few drops garlic juice
bread crumbs**
Stir mixture over low heat until
a little dry and slightly browned.
Drain head of cauliflower, set it
in a shallow pan and cover the
top generously with the bread
crumbs. Make a ridge across the
top with:
green peppers, chopped fine
cross at right angles with
a ridge of
pimiento, chopped fine

Do all this while the cauliflower
is still hot and serve
immediately. This is a festive
way to serve a vegetable with
your holiday meal.
Serves 6

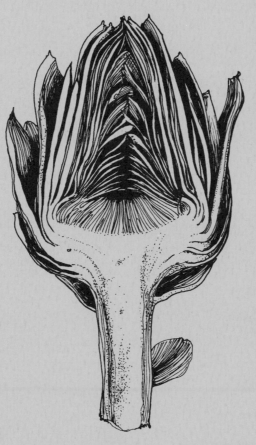

ITALIAN ARTICHOKES

Cook in water for 45 minutes in
saucepan or 10 minutes in
pressure cooker at 15 pounds:
4 large artichokes
1 tablespoon olive oil
1 clove garlic
lemon juice
Remove, drain and separate
leaves enough to sprinkle in the
following mixture.
Heat until browned:
4 tablespoons butter
4 tablespoons olive oil
1 clove garlic, minced very fine
2 cups fine white bread crumbs
Toss with:
1/2 teaspoon herb salt*
1/2 teaspoon dried marjoram
Divide mixture among the
4 artichokes, sprinkling it
down into the leaves. Reheat in
oven to serving temperature.
Serve with:
drawn butter
Serves 4

vegetables

EGGPLANT CAIRO

Simmer until onion is clear,
not browned:
1/2 cup olive oil
3 cloves garlic, minced
1 large onion, chopped coarse
1 green pepper, chopped
1 teaspoon coriander, powdered
1 teaspoon turmeric
1/4 teaspoon cayenne
1 teaspoon fresh ginger root,
minced
1/2 teaspoon powdered ginger
2 bay leaves
(discard after simmering)
Add and stir in well while
cooking so that it will absorb
the oil:
1 medium eggplant, cut into
3/4-inch cubes
Now add:
1 No. 303 can tomatoes, cut up
1 vegetable cube
1 tablespoon brown sugar
Bake in casserole for 1 hour
at 325°. Keep in warm oven
for as much as 1 hour longer, if
possible, to blend flavors. Rice
and fresh yogurt make a good
accompaniment for this dish; or
cottage cheese.
Serves 8

RUSSIAN PEASANT PIE

Mix together:
2 cups all-purpose flour
2 teaspoons salt
Add and with fork press butter
into thin threads:
1/2 pound less 2 tablespoons
butter
Mix butter into flour enough
to distribute it, then make a well
in the mixture and add:
2/3 cup cold buttermilk
Mix just until it all holds
together, then set aside.

Cook in covered kettle until just
done, not mushy:
1/4 pound butter
2 onions, sliced thin
1/2 small head of cabbage,
cored and cut into 1-inch cubes
1 peeled turnip, sliced thin
2 peeled potatos, sliced thin
1 large carrot, sliced very thin
2 cloves garlic, minced
2 teaspoons whole dill seeds
1 teaspoon savory herb blend*
Combine over low heat:
2 tablespoons butter
3 tablespoons flour
Add and cook until thick; stir
constantly with wire whisk:

1 cup milk
1 vegetable cube
Add and mix gently into cooked
vegetables. Chop and add:
1 cup any leftover meat (optional)
The meat is not necessary as the
vegetable mixture is rich and
delicious by itself. Set the mixture
aside to cool.
The pie can be made in 1 large
baking dish or 2 smaller ones,
for this dish can be reheated in
a warm oven and comes out
perfectly. Roll out the dough
very thin and line the bottom and
sides of the baking dish. Fill
with cooled vegetables. (If they
are put in warm they tend to soak
into the bottom crust.) Moisten
the edges of the dough in the
baking dish. Roll out the top
crust very thin and cover the pie.
Make 2 slits in the top to let
out the steam. Bake at 450° for
25 minutes or until top is
nicely brown. If directions have
been followed, the bottom crust
should be nicely browned also.
Serve garnished with yogurt.
This can be a complete meal in
itself, accompanied by a tossed
green salad.
Serves 8

vegetables

LIMA BEAN CASSEROLE

Put into pan with cover:
3 cups dry lima beans
water to cover to 1 inch
above beans
Bring to a boil, turn off heat
and allow beans to stand for
2 hours; then drain and reserve
excess liquid.
Simmer until done but not mushy;
then add to beans:

4 tablespoons olive oil
2 cloves garlic, minced
2 carrots, sliced thin
2 large stalks celery, cut coarse
2 large onions, cut coarse
2 teaspoons fresh ginger
root, minced
Mix together and add:
1 No. 303 can peeled tomatoes,
mashed slightly
2 tablespoons brown sugar
1/4 cup drained bean water
1/4 cup Kikkoman soy sauce
4 sprigs marjoram
4 sprigs basil
2 sprigs thyme
4 sprigs cilantro
4 leaves costmary

or for the fresh herbs,
substitute:
2 teaspoons savory herb blend*
2 teaspoons salt
Bake in casserole for 2 hours at
325° or until beans are
thoroughly done. If beans are not
getting too mushy, a longer
cooking time will blend the
flavors better.
Serves 8 or more

STUFFED BAKED ONIONS

Peel, slice the top off and
scoop out the centers to make
1/2-inch thick shells:
4 very large Spanish onions
Mince:
center parts of onions
Mix with:
1-1/2 cups soft bread crumbs
4 tablespoons butter, melted
1/2 cup chopped walnuts
6 sprigs oregano
2 tablespoons parsley, minced
1/8 teaspoon white pepper
1/4 teaspoon salt
Be sure these ingredients are
well mixed. Fill onion shells
and arrange in baking pan. Blend
and sprinkle over onions:
1/4 cup dry bread crumbs
2 tablespoons butter, melted
1/8 teaspoon basil
Bake in preheated oven at 350°
for 40 minutes or until onions
are tender but not soft.
Garnish with:
minced parsley
paprika
Serves 4

OHIO STEWED CORN

If you are not lucky enough to have your own corn patch, get the freshest corn you can find in the market, allowing:

2 ears of corn for each serving

Keep the corn in the refrigerator until you are ready to prepare it for cooking, then shuck the ears and remove the silks. Stand each ear on end and with a sharp knife slice down, cutting just the top off of each kernel. Do this all around the ear then, with the back of the knife blade, scrape the cob to get the milk and the center of the kernels. Combine in a saucepan:

1/4 cup water
the cut corn
1 tablespoon butter (or more) for each ear
1/4 teaspoon thyme
dash just-ground black pepper

Cover tightly and cook over very low heat for about 5 minutes.

It should just boil, no more, or the starch in the corn will burn on the bottom. Be very careful in this cooking—a scorched taste will be unwelcome. The water should thicken slightly from the starch in the corn. Add and stir in well:

herb salt* to taste

Serve immediately.
Serves 8
As a variation, add:

green pepper, chopped fine

The green pepper will remain slightly crisp, adding delicious flavor and texture.

STEAMED VEGETABLES

Put into frying pan that can be covered:

1/4 pound butter
1 tablespoon mustard seeds

Slowly fry the seeds so they won't burn, until they look a bit brown. Do not overcook them. Then add:

2 carrots, sliced
2 onions, cut coarse
2 stalks celery, cut coarse
1 zucchini, sliced
1 green pepper, chopped

When you can hear the vegetables sizzling, lift the lid slightly on one side and pour in:

1/4 cup hot water

Cover again instantly. The water will provide the steam to begin cooking the vegetables. Turn down the heat to low and continue to cook the vegetables until they are crisp, not mushy. Add:

salt to taste

Serve with brown rice.
Serves 6

vegetables

HERB FRIED POTATOES

This is a version of the German Kartoffel Röesti.
Boil with skins on until just done, but not mushy:

6 potatoes

Peel potatoes and slice thin or put through gricer, coarse cone.

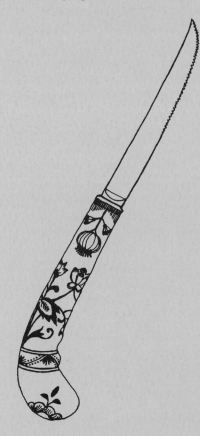

In a large frying pan melt:

1/4 pound butter

Spread potatoes in pan and put on top of them:

1 green pepper, chopped

Grind in mortar and sprinkle over potatoes:

1 sprig thyme
2 sprigs each of basil, marjoram and tarragon
2 leaves costmary
1 teaspoon onion salt
1/2 teaspoon garlic salt

Add:

plenty of chopped parsley

Fry potatoes until golden brown on the bottom. Before turning, dot with:

large pieces of butter

The herbs and peppers will steam then brown lightly when the potatoes are turned. Plenty of butter is the secret. Cook uncovered slowly so they won't burn. It may take 30 minutes. Serve immediately to preserve the crispness of the potatoes.
Serves 6

POTATO MEDLEY

Slice, or put through gricer, coarse cone; then toss together and put into a casserole that can be tightly covered:

2 large potatoes, peeled
2 large white turnips, peeled
2 large onions

Put on top of the vegetables:

thin slices of butter

Cover and bake at 400° until tender, about 30 minutes.

To prepare the sauce, combine over low heat:

1/4 pound butter
6 tablespoons flour

Grind together and add:

1 tablespoon herb salt*
1 teaspoon savory herb blend*

Add, cook and stir until thick:

3 cups milk

Pour the sauce over cooked vegetables and garnish with:

chopped parsley
paprika

Serves 4 - 6

vegetables

SUNCHOKE CASSEROLE

If you're wondering what "sunchoke" means, perhaps you will recognize Jerusalem artichoke as being the name of a native American tuber which was a staple of our Indians long before the white man came to trouble them. This root of the California sunflower is a valuable but not too well-known vegetable, low in starch but very high in protein, delicious in taste and of a wonderful texture, something like water chestnuts. They can be added raw to a mixed salad, sliced thin; served as a buttered cooked vegetable, and, as in the recipe below, combined with other things. Where the name Jerusalem artichoke came from is still questioned, and now the vegetable men have decided to give them a new name—sunchokes.

Cook until clear:
1 clove garlic, minced, in
2 tablespoons butter
2 teaspoons herb salt*

Wash well, being sure to get the dirt out of broken parts (you do not need to peel):
1-1/2 pounds sunchokes, sliced
Combine with:
1 onion, sliced thin
Add to cooked garlic with:
1/4 cup water
Cover. Cook until done, being careful not to overcook as they get mushy very quickly after

they are done. They should be almost dry when finished, with no water to dilute the casserole; watch that they do not burn.

Braise:
1 pound ground chuck
1/2 teaspoon salt
2 tablespoons butter
1 bay leaf
(discard when cooked)
Mix into the braised beef:
1/2 teaspoon marjoram
1/4 teaspoon thyme
a pinch of sage, no more
Mix beef and vegetables together and put into a buttered casserole. Beat together and then pour over the casserole ingredients:
3 whole eggs
2 egg yolks
2 cups milk
Lay on top:
pimiento strips
Bake at 350° until an inserted knife comes out clean, about 30 minutes. Here is a high protein dish that should please everyone, especially when served with corn on the cob.
Serves 6

GREEN SOYBEANS IN SAUCE

Simmer slowly until celery is done but not mushy:
2 large stalks celery, cut coarse
2 tablespoons safflower or other oil
1 tablespoon water
Add:
1 17-ounce can Loma Linda green soybeans
2 tablespoons Kikkoman soy sauce
Simmer gently for 5 minutes.
Serves 4

QUICK CURRIED BEANS

Sauté until clear; do not brown:
1/2 large onion, minced in
2 tablespoons safflower or other oil
Mix in when onion is cooked:
2 teaspoons curry powder
Add and simmer gently for 5 minutes:
1 No. 2-1/2 can prepared baked beans
Serve on toast.
Serves 4

SWISS-STYLE YELLOW WAX BEANS

Prepare by clipping ends and then cutting beans into 1-1/2-inch pieces:
2 pounds yellow wax beans
Cook very slowly until clear:
1 clove garlic, minced
2 tablespoons onion, chopped in
2 tablespoons sweet butter
Mix together in pressure cooker and cook for 5 minutes without pressure cap or in covered pot until tender:
the prepared beans
onion and garlic mixture
1/2 cup water
3/4 teaspoon herb salt*
1/2 teaspoon savory herb blend*
When done the water should be all gone, and perhaps a little more will have to be added during the cooking to keep beans from sticking. Heat together gently to melt cheese:
3 ounces cream cheese
1/2 cup coffee cream
Add melted cheese to beans.
Serves 6

vegetables

COOKING RICE

One cup of raw rice combined with two cups of liquid makes two cups of cooked rice, or four medium-size servings. The two methods of cooking rice I prefer are the Chinese and the Near Eastern.

Chinese Method: Slowly pour the rice into a pot of rapidly boiling salted water, so that the water does not stop boiling as the rice is added. Cover, reduce heat and steam for about 20 minutes. Drain rice in a strainer and rinse with hot water to wash away the starch. Reheat in the oven before serving.

Near Eastern Method: Melt oil or butter in a pan that can be tightly covered. Stir in unwashed rice and salt. Then place the pan over a very hot flame until the grains turn slightly white, but are not browned. Immediately pour boiling water over the rice, stir, cover and place over low heat to simmer for about 20 minutes.

BROWN RICE SUPREME

If you use California brown rice it must be cooked about twice as long as Texas or Louisiana rice because it has a much tougher skin. The shorter cooking time is given here.
Make a rich chicken broth using:
2 cups water
1 pound gizzards
Mince and reserve the gizzards.
Put into a frying pan that can be tightly covered:
2 tablespoons butter or chicken fat
1 cup unwashed brown rice (it must be dry)
Heat until very hot but do not brown, then stir in:
2 cups rich chicken broth, boiling hot
2 chicken soup cubes dissolved in a little broth
the minced gizzards
1/2 green pepper, minced (optional)
Cover immediately and simmer for 1/2 hour or until rice is done. Do not stir. Serve with chicken dishes or with lamb.

GREEN RICE

Heat in skillet that can be
tightly covered:
2 tablespoons oil
**1 cup unwashed white long-grain
rice**
1 teaspoon salt
Prepare and mix together:
1 teaspoon celery leaves, chopped
1/2 green pepper, chopped
1/4 cup parsley, minced
**1/4 cup green onion tops,
chopped fine**
Mix together and stir into
heated rice:
2 cups boiling water
2 drops green coloring
Add chopped vegetables, cover
and simmer until done, about
1/2 hour. Do not uncover while
simmering.

RED RICE

Follow same procedure as in
preceding recipe for green rice,
stirring together:
1 cup long-grain white rice
2 tablespoons oil
1 teaspoon salt
Keeping rice hot, mix together
and stir in:
1 teaspoon paprika
2 pimientos, diced
2 cups boiling water
Cover immediately and simmer
until done, at least 30 minutes.
Do not stir.

SAFFRON RICE

Steep:
1/8 teaspoon saffron in
1/2 cup boiling water
Follow same procedure as with
green rice, stirring together:
1 cup long-grain white rice
2 tablespoons oil
1 teaspoon salt
Add saffron water to:
1-1/2 cups boiling water
Add to rice, cover immediately
and simmer until done.

TURMERIC RICE

Follow same procedure as with
green rice, stirring together:
1 cup long-grain white rice
2 tablespoons oil
1 teaspoon salt
Add and mix in:
1/4 teaspoon turmeric
Keeping rice mixture hot, add
and stir in:
2 cups boiling water
Cover immediately and simmer
until done, at least 30 minutes.
Do not stir.

vegetables

TOFU

It is strange that it has taken Americans so long to discover a most wonderful protein that has been used in China and Japan for centuries. Only recently has it become available in our supermarkets. It is called tofu and is known by other names like bean curd and bean cake. It is made from the milk of the soybean and comes packed and sealed in liquid.

By itself, tofu does not have much flavor and needs to be permeated by the flavors of other vegetables and seasonings; but it is a protein of such great food value and its texture is so marvelous that you will enjoy a feeling of well-being whenever you eat it.

Combinations using tofu are practically unlimited. When combining it with other vegetables, however, you must slice it or cut it into smaller squares and keep these from being broken up too much. In Japan it is often eaten as it is, with only a little soy sauce added.

TOFU SAUTÉ

If tofu is new to you, you might just as well start by trying one of the most difficult ways to prepare it!

Cut into squares and drain on paper toweling:
1 package tofu
Heat in shallow pan:
3 tablespoons oil
With spatula or pancake turner slide tofu squares into the hot oil and brown on both sides. This is difficult because the tofu is so easily broken up. But persevere, persevere, and you will have a crisp, delicious treat. Serve with:
soy sauce and/or
chopped, fried onions
or dream up your own sauce.

TOFU WITH MUSHROOMS

Cook until soft but not mushy:
4 large onions, sliced thin
4 cloves garlic, minced in
6 tablespoons butter
Add and cook on low heat until just soft, stirring frequently:
1 pound mushrooms, sliced
2 green peppers, cut coarse
2 pimientos, diced
Drain and reserve juice from:
1 package tofu
Mix well together:
3 tablespoons cornstarch
juice from tofu
Add to mushroom mixture. Cook until just thickened, then add:
1/2 cup Kikkoman soy sauce
tofu, cut into 1-inch cubes
Let stand about 20 minutes to blend flavors into the tofu. Reheat and serve with rice or millet. Candied kumquats are a good accompaniment.
Serves 8
As a variation add:
2 tablespoons plain yogurt, or
2 leaves French sorrel, minced

TOFU WITH CHINESE CABBAGE

Slice thin diagonally:
4 large leaves Chinese cabbage
Heat in pan that can be covered:
2 tablespoons peanut oil
1 tablespoon water
Add sliced cabbage leaves and cook until just done, not mushy. Drain and cut into cubes:
1 pound tofu
Cook until just done, slightly crisp:
1 onion, sliced thin, in
1/4 cup peanut oil
Add and cook for 3 minutes:
1/2 pound mushrooms, sliced
Add and cook until thick:
1 cup water
3 tablespoons cornstarch
mixed in a little of the water
1/4 cup soy sauce
Combine the cooked cabbage, tofu squares and the mushroom sauce and let stand for a few minutes to blend flavors. Serve with:
steamed rice
Serves 8

vegetables

PAN BROILED MUSHROOMS

Select with care:
3 mushrooms for each serving
They should be the largest you
can find, the russet type if
available. This type has the
most flavor and does not shrink
as the others do. The "skirt"
should be attached tightly to
the stem, for then they are
fresh, not dried out. Wash the
mushrooms well under running
water, scrubbing off embedded
bits of dirt. Do not peel them.
Cut off the stem even with the
bottom of the mushroom; do not
break it off for then a hole
is left in the underside of the
mushroom.
In a frying pan melt a generous
amount of:
sweet butter

Lay mushrooms in the pan, cut
side down. Cover and cook slowly
until the tops feel as soft as
the side of your forearm. When
done on the first side, turn them
with tongs. Put onto each stem:
2 or 3 drops Worcestershire sauce
good dash of herb salt*
Continue cooking under cover
until the second side is gently
brown.
Meanwhile, toast:
1 slice of bread for each serving
Spread generously with:
butter which has been lightly
seasoned with
garlic powder
Place the buttered toast on
a hot platter. Lift out each
mushroom without spilling
the juice in the cap and turn
it over on the toast so the
juice will soak into it. Pour
remaining pan juices over the
mushrooms. These mushrooms are
also delicious served on
steamed rice.

OLIVE-TOMATO APPETIZER

Prepare a marinade by mixing
together:
3/4 cup olive oil
3 tablespoons wine vinegar
juice of 1/2 lemon
10 turns of the pepper mill
Pour marinade over:
3 medium cans pitted black
olives, drained
Marinate olives in refrigerator
for 5 hours. One hour before
serving, mix in gently:
2 cups cherry tomatoes,
sliced in half
Continue to chill until ready
to serve. Drain off marinade and
serve in large relish bowl
placed in crushed ice. Have
toothpicks available. This is
excellent served with
champagne cocktails.

vegetables

RIJSTTAFEL

One of our friends in Ojai, Melani von Gelder, lived on a tea plantation in Java so large that the employees had their own village numbering 35,000 persons. She learned their way of cooking the Indonesian dish called rijsttafel, which means "rice table." Here are some of the things served under this famous name. We had it in Amsterdam at the Bali, one of the most famous restaurants of this type in the world. Our dinner consisted of 25 different dishes and they were all delicious. Some of these recipes follow on the next pages.

vegetables

RICE FOR RIJSTTAFEL

According to the recipe on
(page 76), prepare.
a large quantity of rice
In Java, they always use white
rice, but you can substitute brown
if you choose. When the rice is
cooked, toss lightly with:
**slivered almonds, lightly fried
in butter
thin green beans, cooked**
The Javanese use "3-foot beans"
(they really are about that long),
cut into 4-inch lengths. Heap
up the rice on a very large
platter and place it in the
middle of the table.
Serve the following dishes
with the rice.

NASI GORENG

Sauté:
**1 cup mushrooms, sliced
1 onion, minced, in
4 tablespoons peanut oil**
When onion is cooked, add and
continue to cook 5 more minutes:
**1 cup any type cooked meat
1/2 cup tomato ketchup (or to
taste)
1/4 teaspoon salt**
This is poured over the rice at
one end of the large platter
on which the rice is served.

BOEME

Cook until just done, then drain:
1 package thin noodles
Fry lightly:
**2 cups mushrooms, sliced
2 green onions, with tops,
cut up, in
2 tablespoons peanut oil**
Add cooked noodles and:
**1 10-ounce package frozen peas
1/4 teaspoon salt**
Toss lightly and reheat to
defrost peas. Keep warm in bowl
to be set alongside rice. In Java
the vegetables are often served
cold because of the warm climate.

GADO GADO

Sauté lightly, just enough to
wilt the vegetables:
**1 pound fresh spinach, torn
slightly
1 pound bean sprouts
1 green onion, chopped fine, in
butter or peanut oil**
Prepare a sauce by sautéing very
slowly to prevent burning:
**1/2 cup peanut butter
1 teaspoon sugar
1/4 teaspoon fresh grated ginger**
Pour sauce over vegetables and
serve in a separate dish
alongside the rice platter.

TRIEKADEL

Mix together well:
1 16-ounce can whole kernel corn, drained
1/4 cup parsley, minced
1/2 pound spinach leaves, chopped
1 cup Cheddar cheese, grated
1 green pepper, chopped
1/8 teaspoon powdered cloves
1/8 teaspoon grated nutmeg
3 eggs, beaten
1/2 cup canned mushroom soup
rolled oats, sufficient to thicken
batter for griddle frying
Heat and grease griddle. Drop on a spoonful of batter, brown on one side and then turn to brown on the other.

To serve this as a casserole, add and mix the following into the batter:
1/2 cup sweet pickles, chopped
1 small can pimientos, chopped
1/2 cup tomato wedges
Pour mixture into buttered casserole and bake at 375° until top browns. Serve, either the pancakes or casserole with the following peanut sauce.

PEANUT SAUCE

This is served on many vegetables, which have been cooked, drained and chilled. The dressing should also be cold.
Sauté:
2 onions, minced, in
2 tablespoons peanut oil
Add and mix in well:
1 teaspoon brown sugar
1 tablespoon lime juice
1/4 cup chunky peanut butter
1 cup coconut milk
dash salt

LEMON CURD

This Indonesian lemon jelly is served for dessert.
Beat together for 1 minute:
2 eggs
2 egg yolks
rind of 4 lemons, grated
2/3 cup lemon juice
1/2 pound butter, melted
Pour this filling into prebaked pie shell. Cover top with:
rum-flavored whipped cream
Serve ice cold.
Other suitable desserts to serve with rijsttafel are bananas flambé or vanilla ice cream with hot ginger sauce and shredded fresh coconut.

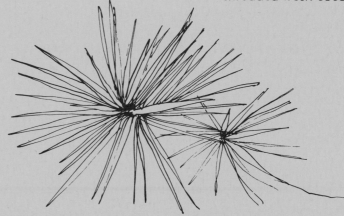

beef

"It is very nice to think
The world is full of
   meat and drink"
            R. L. Stevenson

A few years ago I was being taken around Rome by a friend, to one restaurant after another. There were no steak houses such as we have in this country and I said to her, "I am going to come over here and open a steak house." "Where," she said, "will you get the steak? There is no aged beef in Rome that I know anything about."

That was some years ago and things may have changed, but generally in Europe the favorite meat of the bovine animal is young, tender white veal, which we are not so accustomed to in this country. Though in Britain beef is standard on the menu, it is not aged to our taste and is therefore apt to be tough and is customarily sliced very thin in serving. So, in an American restaurant we ask for an English cut if we want thin slices of roast beef and for a Diamond Jim Brady cut if we want an extra thick slice.

Beef is a strong-flavored meat so one of the best herbs to go along with it is bay leaf. Black pepper and horseradish are also favorites of long standing. (What British housewife would serve boiled beef without its accompanying horseradish!) A mixture such as our own herb blend for meat is acceptable and of course chives and garlic are liked by almost everyone. Many beefeaters do not want anything at all on their beef, they so much like its flavor au naturel.

84

TOURNEDOS BÉARNAISE

The tournedos is the finest cut
of beef—an 8-inch piece of the
center of the tenderloin strip
is used. The cuts are usually
1/2- to 3/4-inch thick, and
1-1/2 inches thick if you
like your steak very rare. Be
sure that you get this cut
from your butcher, not
the ends of the strip.

The steaks are to be fried
very quickly, therefore they
should be at room temperature
before being put into the pan.
Heat a heavy pan, put in it
enough butter to fry the steaks
(only sweet butter should be
used), and add the steaks
immediately so that the butter
will not burn. Fry quickly just
until lightly browned, turn
and salt lightly with herb salt.
Lay pan-broiled large mushrooms
(see page 80) on each steak.
Serve on hot plates accompanied
by a baked potato topped with
green onion butter. Serve with
a bowl of béarnaise sauce to
spoon over the steak and
mushrooms. What a delicious
combination of flavors!

TOURNEDOS ROSSINI

(This is another famous way
to serve the tenderloin filet.)
Have each serving of steak cut
1-1/2-inches thick. Fry as
above to the desired doneness
and put on a hot plate with
the broiled mushrooms, one to
each steak. On top of the
mushroom put a 1/2-inch slice
of paté de foie gras.
(The paté will not slice
unless it is chilled. Roll it in
waxed paper, chill and slice.)
Serve with béarnaise sauce.

beef

TOURNEDOS ZOIA

Slice in 6 8-ounce slices:
3 pounds tenderloin filet
Braise until done but not
too brown:
1/4 pound butter
3 cups onions, sliced thin
Add and continue to cook
until just done:
1 pound mushrooms, sliced thin
Grind in mortar:
1/2 teaspoon meat herbs*
1/2 teaspoon herb salt*
Mix with:
**1 tablespoon beef
concentrate (Bovril)**
Add to mushrooms and onions.
Mix together:
1/2 cup whole milk
**1 cup béchamel (or rich
cream) sauce**
1-1/2 cups sour cream
1/2 teaspoon Kitchen Bouquet
Add to mushroom and onion
mixture and stir in well. Reheat
but do not cook as it tends
to curdle.
Fry the beef filets lightly
in a heavy iron pan, in sweet
butter. Season with herb salt
and serve on hot serving plates
with the sauce spooned over
each slice.

This is an excellent dish to
serve if guests are late. The
sauce keeps well heated and the
steaks can be cooked at the
last moment, when the
guests arrive.
Serves 6

RYE STEAK

This recipe was given to me by Nancy Adams, our hostess at the Ranch House.

Using a heavy iron skillet, sauté:
2 porterhouse steaks
Do not cook too much, as they will cook more in the sauce. Put the braised steaks aside on a platter, keeping them warm. In the skillet where the steaks were cooked, sauté gently until golden brown:
4 green onions, white parts only, minced
Add and mix in:
1 tablespoon BV beef extract
Now stir in and mix well:
1/2 cup rye whiskey
juice of 1/2 lemon
Simmer about 5 minutes then taste. If it is too salty, thin with a little water but keep in mind that it must be rather salty to flavor the steaks. Put the steaks back in the pan and cook to your taste. Don't overcook them.
Serves 2

ITALIAN BUTTER-FRIED BEEF

One of the most interesting rotisseries I have seen was in Rome. In the wall at one end of the room was set an iron grate filled with red-hot coals. In front of it were the roasting pieces of beef on their turning rods sizzling appetizingly. This was the middle of summer and the weather was very hot. To protect the diners from the heat a wall of thick glass had been erected and flowing down this wall was a steady stream of water, lowering the temperature as much by suggestion as by fact.
The beef was served thinly sliced, with a wedge of lemon, and accompanied by a large green salad dressed with plenty of olive oil and vinegar, an excellent meal for a hot evening.

You can serve your own version of this dish. Have your butcher cut the tenderloin in very thin slices. Get out your old iron frying pan and put in it some sweet butter (which doesn't burn as quickly as the salted type). When the butter is about to burn, put in the beef slices and stir them around only enough to just cook them. Add a sprinkling of herb salt.* The beef slices should be pink. Serve them immediately, right from the skillet. Have handy a pepper mill and a plate of lemon wedges, the only seasoning necessary for this type of beef.

GINGERED TOP SIRLOIN STEAK

Don't skimp on the quality of the steak—nothing but the aged sirloin will do. Cook in your favorite way, over intensely hot coals or in buttered pan. Cook one side, turn, and immediately sprinkle on a mixture of finely chopped fresh ginger root, a little salt and some freshly ground black pepper. Lightly press the seasoning into the meat with a spatula. The amount of fresh ginger used will depend on your liking for this seasoning. A squeeze of lemon may also be added.

beef

PRIME RIB WITH YORKSHIRE PUDDING

A reason for serving this fine
cut of beef, besides its being
traditional "Sunday food," is
to have that delicious crusty
pastry, Yorkshire pudding,
as an accompaniment.
Does anyone have to be told how
to cook this most popular
roast? There are actually a
number of ways to prepare it and
perhaps you might like to
try this one:
Have ready in whatever size
you need:
prime-rib roast
Rub the surface of the roast with:
herb salt* and
freshly ground black pepper
Roast in a 325° oven,
allowing 20 minutes per pound
(15 minutes if you like the
roast very rare). When done,
remove the roast and use the
drippings in the Yorkshire
pudding recipe which follows. If
the roast is too rare for one
of your guests, dip the slice in
the hot juice for a minute or
two, until it is the desired
color. Skim and reserve fat
and juice.

YORKSHIRE PUDDING

My maternal grandmother came from Sheffield, England, and when I was young she did much of the family cooking. I remember especially her Sunday dinner of roast beef and Yorkshire pudding. The roast was well done so there would be plenty of juice to make gravy. It was cooked in a black iron pan about 10 by 14 inches which grandmother called a dripping pan.

When done the meat was removed from the pan and kept warm. The "drippings" were poured from the pan, then the fat was skimmed and returned to it. Enough pudding was made to fill the pan to about an inch in depth. While the pudding was baking a rich brown gravy was made by adding water to the juice and the right amount of flour, salt and French capers.

The pudding was cut into squares, loaded with gravy and served with slices of beef and a vegetable, usually peas—and we would enjoy a traditional English Sunday dinner. The children tried to wangle the corner pieces of the pudding because they were so brown and crusty.

At the Ranch House we make individual puddings, each one brown and crusty, and fill them with the beef juice. Here is how it is done:

Prepare four medium-sized Pyrex baking cups by brushing them with fat from the roast. Put the greased cups into the oven for at least 15 minutes with the oven quite hot, 400°.

While cups are heating, mix in blender for 1/2 minute:

2 eggs
1 cup pie flour
1 cup milk
3/4 teaspoon salt

Take cups from oven and pour in each a little fat (not too much). Fill each cup about 3/4 full of batter and return to a 400° oven. Bake until the puddings rise up high and take on a wonderful brown color. Usually there is a hole in the center of each baked pudding. Mix in a little water and add to beef juice:

1 beef extract cube

As you put each pudding on the serving plate, fill the hole with the beef juice mixture. (If the baking cup has been properly cured by the heating, the pudding will lift our easily.)
Serves 4

beef

BEEF STROGANOFF

When we reopened the Ranch House and started serving meat, I had not eaten meat since my early youth and the flavors were almost forgotten. There I was, a reformed vegetarian, faced with learning how to prepare meat dishes. As a start, I decided I would achieve my own versions of three entrees, the names of which had attracted me: beef stroganoff, chicken cacciatore and veal scaloppini. Boldly I chose the beef stroganoff first and called a friend in the Ojai Valley whose reputation as a cook is attested by all who have had the good fortune to enjoy her hospitality. She suggested recipes and I read others. Then I put them all aside and started to experiment. Having read that the meat must be fried quickly and then sour cream added, I learned that part of the secret was to have the iron skillet very hot and to use suet

instead of butter for the frying. Butter burns too easily, and the beef must be cooked rapidly, with great heat or the meat juices will run out into the pan and the meat will be boiled instead of fried.

The day I started on the stroganoff, I had made béchamel sauce, and it was cooling on the back of the stove. Since it had such a wonderful flavor, I added some of it along with the sour cream. Then I added fried mushrooms, a little tomato paste and other seasonings. The whole concoction was then heated in the double boiler. It is very important to let it mature for at least an hour, I have found, so that the flavors will blend completely.

Since I had never tasted beef stroganoff, I had only my own ideas to go on, and so could not imitate. As I concocted the dish for the next three or four times, I adjusted the proportions of

the ingredients until I felt it was as good as I could make it. Here is the recipe as we now serve it:

Slice into pieces about 1-1/2-inches long and 1/2-inch wide, and brown quickly in iron skillet greased with suet:
1-1/2 pounds beef, tenderloin or tips
As meat is browned, put it in a double boiler to keep hot.
Sauté in butter:
4 ounces mushrooms, sliced
dash of herb salt*
Mix well and add to mushrooms:
10 ounces sour cream
10 ounces béchamel sauce (page 24)
1 tablespoon tomato paste
1/2 teaspoon salt
1/8 teaspoon black pepper, fresh ground
Add mixture to braised beef in double boiler and allow to mature for 1 hour. Then heat for 15 minutes and serve with rice.
Serves 4

BEEF A LA MODE

You can serve a large prime-rib roast without wondering what you can do with the leftovers. Some people like this better than the prime-rib dinner. Cut into 1-inch squares, removing all fat:

1 pound cooked prime-rib beef

Cook until smooth:

1 cup beef juice from pan drippings
2 tablespoons flour

Add and stir in well:

1 cup béchamel sauce
2 teaspoons beef concentrate
1/4 teaspoon Kitchen Bouquet
1/4 teaspoon lemon juice

When sauce is well blended add:

1 cup cooked small white onions, drained
1 cup cooked tiny carrots (optional)
the cubed beef

Reheat to serving temperature and allow to stand at this temperature for at least 30 minutes to blend flavors before serving. Serve in large casserole garnished with thin sliced mushrooms and a large dollop of sour cream. Accompany this dish with boiled potatoes or buttered noodles, and wedges of tomatoes and slices of green pepper.
Serves 6

beef

BEEF BALI HAI

A few years ago in Paris a friend of mine took me to meet a man who had two restaurants, one for students located near the Sorbonne and very inexpensive, and another located on the Left Bank, for knowledgeable Frenchmen and lucky tourists like myself. The owner, Mr. So was Chinese, born in Viet Nam. One of his dishes was called Pork of the Five Perfumes, and I remember a soup made with shredded crabmeat, plenty of rice and Chinese parsley. The broth was chicken and the blend was perfect.

When I came home I tried to duplicate some of his dishes. One of them I proposed to call Beef Viet Nam but the waitresses would not go along with that so we call it Beef Bali Hai.

Put into small frying pan that can be covered tightly:

2 tablespoons butter
Heat to browning point and then add and cover tightly:
5 large green onions, cut diagonally
1/2 green pepper, cut into thin strips
In about 10 seconds, no more, add, pouring around the edge of the lid so that it does not have to be lifted:
4 tablespoons hot water.
Steam the vegetables for 1/2 minute **only.**
Mix together and heat, stirring until thickened:

2 cups chicken broth
1 teaspoon cinnamon
3 tablespoons ginger syrup
2 teaspoons lemon juice
4 vegetable cubes well dissolved in a little water
4 sprigs of wild anise, chopped fine
1 tablespoon cornstarch dissolved in a little water
Combine with steamed onions and green peppers, then add:
2 pounds cooked prime-rib beef, diced
1/2 cup pignolia nuts
Reheat and serve over turmeric rice.
Serves 8

beef

BRANDIED BEEF
(Beef Bourguignon)

Cut into 1/2-inch cubes:
1/2 pound salt pork
Fry cubes in heavy iron pan
until fat is cooked out and
cubes are golden brown; then
remove cubes and save them.
Cut into 1-inch cubes:
**6 pounds round bone beef roast
(shoulder of beef)**
Brown beef cubes well on all
sides in pork fat.
Put pork and beef cubes in
pressure cooker or heavy pot
and add:
1/2 cup good brandy
Cover immediately while hot and
refrigerate for 24 hours.
Add following ingredients to
marinated beef and simmer,
covered, in heavy pan until
tender (or at 15 pounds pressure
for 12 minutes):
1 cup water
**2 tablespoons beef concentrate
(or 6 beef cubes)**
2 cloves garlic, minced
1/2 teaspoon meat herb blend*

3 bay leaves
3/4 cup dry Burgundy
1/4 teaspoon fresh ground pepper
When done, drain juice and add
to it enough water to make
3 cups. Thicken with:
4 tablespoons flour
Add to meat:
2 cups small whole cooked carrots
2 cups small whole cooked onions
Pour gravy over meat and
vegetables. Reheat and let stand
30 minutes to blend flavors.
Serves 10

SAUERBRATEN
WITH NOODLES

Combine in a stone crock:
1 pint vinegar
1/2 cup red wine
1 cup water
Add, being sure the liquid
covers it completely:
5 pounds chuck beef
Lay on, or push into the beef:
8 bay leaves
12 peppercorns
8 whole cloves
Marinate beef for one week in
refrigerator, turning every day

so that all sides of the meat
will be exposed to the marinade.
(Do not add salt or ground
pepper at this time, because
salt would draw out all the
juices of the meat and make it
dry.) After 1 week, remove
and drain.
Put into heavy pot or pressure
cooker and heat very hot:
4 tablespoons fat
Sear beef well on all sides;
then spread over it:
2 cloves garlic, minced
7 turns of pepper mill
3 large carrots, sliced thin
3 large onions, cut coarse
**4 tablespoons beef extract,
salted variety (or 12 cubes)**
2 cups marinade from crock
1 cup water
Cook, covered, very
slowly for several hours until
beef is tender or for 12 minutes
at 15 pounds in pressure cooker
(cool and remove cap immediately,
to prevent overcooking). Thicken
liquid with flour for gravy and
salt to taste. Serve with cooked
noodles and gravy.
Serves 8

93

beef

FONDUE BOURGUIGNONNE

This famous Swiss fondue is served everywhere in Switzerland. It is not too difficult to prepare and can be one of the most festive dishes that can be imagined for a party.

You will need an alcohol stove and a metal pan to set over it, or the regular fondue casserole with its own heat; long wooden-handled forks with sharp tines to spear strips of beef, one for each guest; and for each guest a supply of wooden skewers.

Have your butcher cut into strips, 2-inches wide and 1/4-inch thick: **beef tenderloin, 1/2 pound or more per person**

Slice the tenderloin strips into 1/2-inch wide pieces. And make sure it is at room temperature when ready to serve.

Put the following mixture in the fondue pot or pan so that the pot is about 2/3 full:
one part butter
two parts peanut oil

In the kitchen preheat the butter and oil until it is very hot and then place it over a high alcohol flame at the table to keep it hot. Place before each guest, a dish of the tenderloin strips, ringed by little bowls of any of the following sauces. Each guest cooks his pieces of beef, one at a time in the hot oil, using the long-handled fork; then the cooked meat is taken off the fork with the skewer, dipped into any one of the sauces and popped into his mouth.

SAUCES FOR BOURGUIGNONNE

Béarnaise: (page 25)

Russian: Mix together mayonnaise and catsup, to just the right flavor.

Mustard Mayonnaise: Mix dry mustard into mayonnaise.

Creamed Horseradish: Mix together sweet cream, dash of herb salt*, 1 teaspoon lemon juice, good sharp horseradish.

Mushroom Sauce: Allow at least one large mushroom for each person. Mince mushrooms, add herb salt* to taste, fry in butter until tender—a couple of minutes only—in a covered pan to preserve moisture. Sprinkle lightly with flour, stirring rapidly to prevent lumping, and cook to thick sauce consistency; mix in well a few drops of lemon juice.

Mayonnaise Oriental: Melt in a shallow pan, 2 tablespoons butter. Add 1 teaspoon curry powder, 1 minced green onion. Cook covered until onion is done. Stir this into 1 cup mayonnaise. Add and stir in: 1/2 teaspoon apricot jam, 1 teaspoon lemon juice. Mix well. Serves 6

Green Onions: Chop very fine and sprinkle lightly with herb salt.*

FONDUE BACCHUS

This is served like the
Bourguignonne, except that the
meat, cut in strips like the beef,
is:
veal tenderloin, well pounded
Cooked in:
white wine,
heated and kept very hot.
When heating the wine in the
kitchen, put into it:
**1 onion, peeled and stuck with
3 or 4 cloves**
Remove the onion when the wine
is taken to the table.

beef

BEEF ITALIANO

Cut for broiling (1/2 pound per portion):
4 pounds top sirloin
Braise until just done:
1 minced garlic clove in
2 tablespoons olive oil
Add and cook until tender (or for 2 minutes at 15 pounds in a pressure cooker):
1 onion, sliced thin
1/2 green pepper, sliced thin
6 sprigs oregano
2 sprigs fresh tarragon
6 sprigs basil
2 teaspoons Italian sauce
(page 28) optional
Slice medium thick:
4 cups fresh mushrooms
Toss lightly in:
2 tablespoons lemon juice
Drain mushrooms, retaining lemon juice, and sprinkle lightly with:
herb salt*

Add mushrooms to vegetables and cook for 1 minute only in covered pan. Mix together and cook until thickened; then add to vegetables:
1 cup water
1-1/2 teaspoons beef concentrate
lemon juice from mushrooms
3 tablespoons flour mixed in
a little of the water
Broil the steak and then spread the vegetable mixture over it. Serve with lemon wedges to be squeezed over each portion.
Serves 8

SAVORY MEAT LOAF

Mash together in a pan:
1/2 cup sunflower seeds
2 small onions, minced
2 eggs
2 tablespoons horseradish
1 teaspoon prepared mustard
1/2 green pepper, minced
1/4 cup tomato ketchup
1/2 teaspoon meat herb blend*
1/8 teaspoon black pepper
1-1/2 teaspoons salt
1/4 pound sausage meat
1/2 cup stuffed olives
(optional but very good)
Then add:
2 cups soft bread cubes
1/2 cup coffee cream
Add and mix well by squeezing
with the hands:
2 pounds ground chuck beef
Put into baking pan and press
down lightly, then pour over it:
1/4 cup rich chicken stock
Bake at 375° for about 1 hour,
or until done.
Serves 8 - 10

LASAGNE

Prepare as directed on package:
lasagne noodles
Wash in cold water to remove
excess starch then drain well.
Cook until soft:
3 cloves garlic, minced
2 onions, minced in
4 tablespoons olive oil
Add and continue to cook gently
for 5 minutes:
1 green pepper, cut fine
1 cup mushrooms, sliced
2 bay leaves
2 teaspoons herb salt*
1 teaspoon tomato herb blend*
Add and cook for 1 minute:
2 6-ounce cans tomato paste
2 cups hot water
1 pound ground meat
Discard bay leaves.
Put layer of cooked noodles in
a baking dish which has been
greased with:
olive oil
Spoon some of the sauce over
the noodles, then cover with:
Mozzarella cheese
Ricotta cheese (or cottage
cheese)
Continue these layers of
noodles, sauce and cheese. Bake
at 350° for 30 to 45 minutes
or until sauce begins to bubble
at the edges and the cheese is
melted. Serve with tossed green
salad.
Serves 8

beef

SWEDISH MEATBALLS

Mix well together:
2 ounces pork sausage,
seasoned by butcher
3/4 cup onion, chopped fine
3 whole eggs
3/8 teaspoon nutmeg
3/8 teaspoon fresh ground pepper
1/8 teaspoon powdered cardamon
1/8 teaspoon savory herb blend*
1/2 tablespoon salt
3 cloves garlic, minced fine
Toast and cut up fine:
2 slices white bread
Dissolve bread in:
3/8 cup coffee cream
Add this and the sausage
and herb mixture to:
2-1/2 pounds ground beef
Mix well, squeezing with the
hands; then form into small
balls. Keep balls small so they
will cook thoroughly. Fry them
in oil or butter until lightly
browned on all sides.
Put meatballs in cooking kettle
and add:
3/8 cup Burgundy
1/2 cup water
2 tablespoons chopped parsley
Cook 1/2 hour, then drain off
juice into another pot and
add to it:
3/4 cup sour cream
1/2 tablespoon beef extract
1/8 cup Burgundy
1/2 cup water mixed with
1-1/2 tablespoons flour
1/4 teaspoon Kitchen Bouquet
Cook this sauce until thick and
smooth, stirring well to avoid
curdling sour cream. Pour onto
meatballs and simmer very gently
for about 20 minutes. Do not boil.
Serves 6

BURGERED RICE

Put in frying pan that can be
tightly covered:
4 tablespoons butter or
margarine
1 onion, sliced thin
1/2 green pepper, cut in
small cubes
1/4 teaspoon herb salt*
Cook until onion is clear then
add and brown:
1/2 pound hamburger
Add; then heat until very hot:
1/4 teaspoon marjoram
3 large sprigs parsley, minced
1/8 teaspoon black pepper
1/4 teaspoon garlic salt
1 pinch dill seeds
1/2 cup unwashed white rice
Mix and bring to boil:
1 cup water
1-1/2 teaspoons beef base
Add boiling water to burger
mixture, cover and let simmer
for 25 minutes.
Serves 4

GYPSY BEEF WITH NOODLES

Mix together and cook until
partly clear but not done:
1-1/2 cups onions, minced fine
2 cloves garlic, minced, in
2 tablespoons fat
Remove to mixing bowl and add:
1 cup cooked rice
1/2 teaspoon dill seeds
3-1/2 teaspoons salt
1/2 teaspoon black pepper
1/4 teaspoon meat herb blend*
1 pound seasoned sausage meat
Mix well and add:
3 eggs
5 pounds ground beef
Knead with hands until mixture
is thoroughly blended.
Put into large kettle with
tight cover:
10 unbroken outer leaves of
large cabbage heads
1 cup water
2 tablespoons vinegar
Steam until leaves wilt and can
be easily folded; then lay leaves
on board. Divide meat mixture
into 10 equal portions.
Fold leaves around meat,
wrapping securely, and tie
across each way with string.
Place in baking dish which can
be tightly covered.
Cook for 5 minutes in
covered pan:
1/2 cup water
5 stalks celery, sliced
3 large sprigs parsley, minced
1 tablespoon sugar
6 tablespoons vinegar
1/2 teaspoon salt
1/4 teaspoon black pepper
Remove from heat and stir in:
3 tablespoons tomato paste
Spoon sauce over cabbage rolls.
Bake at 350° for 1 hour or
until done.
Top with sour cream and serve
with boiled noodles mixed with
braised, chopped green onions,
chopped parsley and plenty of
butter.
Serves 10

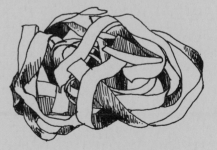

beef

AVOCADO MEAT LOAF

Mix together well:
1 egg, well beaten
1 pound ground round steak
2 tablespoons onion, minced fine
2 tablespoons celery tops,
chopped fine
4 tablespoons tomato ketchup
1-1/2 teaspoons salt
1 cup soft bread crumbs
1 avocado, peeled and
cubed finely
2 tablespoons parsley, chopped
This amount will just fill a
12-hole muffin tin, well greased.
Bake in very hot oven, 400°, for
20 minutes. Do not overcook, as
an acid taste will develop
from the avocado.

To prepare gravy for this dish,
cook until clear:
1 tablespoon onion, minced in
1 tablespoon butter
Brown in dry pan, stirring
constantly:
4 tablespoons ordinary white
flour
(Do not allow it to
get too brown or scorch.)
Add and mix well, then cool:
2 tablespoons butter
Add and mix well, then cook
until thickened:
cleared onions
1 cup water
1 beef or vegetable cube
1 tablespoon shredded
Cheddar cheese
dash fresh ground pepper
1/2 teaspoon Worcestershire
sauce
few drops lime or lemon juice
Add after gravy has thickened:
1/2 avocado, peeled and
finely cubed
Gravy should be brown in color
if the flour was done properly.
A small amount of chopped parsley
may be added if desired. Do not
overheat after adding avocado,
or an acid taste will develop.
Serves 6

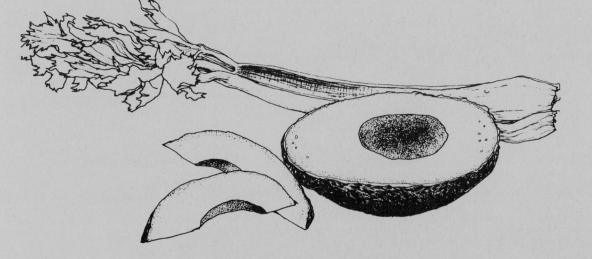

HERBS FOR CHICKEN

"When I eat alone I feel like
a seminarian being punished."
—Pope John XXIII

Such a tremendous variety of
seasonings can be used with
chicken, it is simpler to start
off with the warning that there
are a few strong herbs, such as
sage and rosemary, that one
should use with caution. Cooks
who like to experiment have a
bouquet of flavoring combinations
at their command, needing only
to keep in mind that one must
maintain the balance of the
herbs when using more than one
so that one herb does not
overpower another.

The herbs that go best with
chicken are the milder ones
such as sweet marjoram, basil,
thyme, celery, onion, lovage,
costmary, parsley, pineapple
sage, lemon verbena, a little
lemon balm and chervil and
summer savory in moderation.
One can use sweet things for
flavoring like fruit, or tart
things like tomatoes,
vegetables, green peppers,
olives; then there is the world
of wines to enhance these
flavors. Cordials and liqueurs
are excellent flavoring
diversions for this elegant
meat. Just keep in mind that
the meat itself is of a
delicate flavor and the light
touch is indicated.
If your recipe calls for
cutting the chicken into pieces
for baking or frying, the first
thing to do with the pieces is
to brown them quickly and
lightly in butter or half butter
and half peanut or olive oil to
seal in the juices. If not
treated in this way, the chicken
can be very dry, especially
the white meat.

chicken

CHICKEN POACHED IN CHAMPAGNE

When I began to think about meat dishes to add to our menu after we reopened the Ranch House, the idea of adding the magical taste of champagne to the delicate flavor of chicken intrigued me. I began experimenting, trying various combinations of ingredients and various types of champagne. I found that for cooking the best champagne to use is an inexpensive strong-flavored type; such a wine will best impart the exciting champagne flavor to the dish.

Cook until cleared:
1 onion, minced, in
2 tablespoons butter
Add and cook 1 minute:
5 mushrooms, sliced
Grind in mortar:
1 teaspoon salt
4 lemon verbena leaves
3 mint leaves
4 sprigs marjoram
4 sprigs thyme
1/2 cup chopped parsley
1 clove garlic, minced
1/8 teaspoon pepper
Add herbs to onion mixture and mix with:
3/4 cup champagne, just uncorked
The bubbling process of the champagne while mixing imparts extra flavor to the sauce
Brown lightly in butter:
2 chickens, cut in serving pieces
(Use no flour.)
Lay chicken pieces in pan that can be tightly covered; pour champagne mixture over chicken and marinate for 4 hours; then simmer—do not boil— for 1 hour. Remove chicken and thicken sauce with flour.
Serves 4

CHICKEN MANDARIN

Cut into serving pieces:
2 chickens
Mix together:
1/2 cup flour
1 teaspoon salt
1/4 teaspoon black pepper
Put flour mixture and chicken
pieces into paper bag and shake
until chicken is well coated
with flour. Brown chicken in:
butter
Remove chicken to shallow baking
pan that can be tightly covered.
Mix together and pour over chicken
juice from 1 11-ounce can
of mandarin oranges
1/3 cup Kikkoman soy sauce
1/4 cup firmly packed brown sugar
1/2 teaspoon mace
Bake chicken at 350° for
40 minutes, basting twice with
sauce from pan. Remove from
oven, baste with sauce and
arrange over chicken:
mandarin orange pieces
Return to oven and bake
20 minutes longer. Serve hot
with rice.
Serves 6

CHICKEN CERISE

Cut into serving pieces:
4 chickens
Fry until lightly brown in:
half butter, half peanut oil
Lay pieces in pan that can be
tightly covered and sprinkle
lightly with:
herb salt*
Mix together then pour around
the edges of the pan, so that
the herb salt will not be
washed off:
juice from 1 No. 2-1/2 can of
dark sweet cherries
1/2 cup Cherry Kijafa wine
4 tablespoons lemon juice
4 drops red food coloring (only 4)
Cover pan and bake at 400°
until done, about 40 to 45
minutes. Drain juice and skim
fat from it. Taste juice for
tartness; it may need a little
more lemon juice. Boil gently
until reduced by one half.
Adjust seasoning by adding:
chicken base concentrate
Dissolve in a little water
and stir in:
2 tablespoons cornstarch
When thickened, add cherries
and serve over chicken pieces.
Serves 8

CHICKEN ROMANOFF

Prepare cheese sauce by
heating in double boiler:
1-1/4 cups béchamel sauce
(page 24)
1-1/4 cups coffee cream
1 cup very sharp Cheddar
cheese, grated
1/2 teaspoon Worcestershire
sauce
dash herb salt*
dash cayenne pepper
(not too much)
1/2 tablespoon sherry
Place in baking dish or pan:
8 servings of chicken or
turkey slices
sprinkle with herb salt*
Place on each serving, cut
side down:
1/2 cooked broccoli spear,
cut lengthwise
Top with:
mornay sauce (page 24)
and bake at 350° until
sauce begins to bubble. Garnish
with minced parsley and paprika.
Serves 8

chicken

CHICKEN SOUBISE

Cut into serving pieces:
2 chickens
Fry until lightly brown in:
half butter, half peanut oil
Lay pieces in pan that can be
tightly covered. Lay over
chicken:
1/2 cup onion, sliced paper thin
Sprinkle on:
**1/2 cup mushrooms, chopped fine
herb salt* (lightly)**
Pour around sides of pan:
1/4 cup white wine
Cover pan and bake at 400°
until done, about 40 minutes.
Drain and reserve liquid.

Prepare sauce Soubise as follows:
1 cup onions, sliced very thin
Cook onions for 10 minutes,
no more, in:
**rich beef stock (can be made
by mixing 1 teaspoon beef base
in 1/2 cup water)**
Drain onions and discard liquid.
Add to drained onions and cook

slowly for 5 minutes without
browning as this is to be a
white sauce:
1 tablespoon butter
1/2 teaspoon herb salt*
Mix together and add to onions,
stirring well:
**1/2 cup mornay sauce (page 24)
enough liquid from chicken to
give the sauce
a proper consistency**
Serve sauce over chicken.
Garnish with watercress and
paprika.
Serves 4

CHICKEN TOLEDO

Cut into serving pieces:
2 chickens
Fry until lightly brown in:
olive oil
Lay pieces in pan that can be
tightly covered. Sprinkle with:
herb salt*
Spread over chicken:

1 small onion, sliced paper thin
Mix together and spread
over this:
1 large green pepper, cubed
**1/2 can pitted ripe olives,
cut into fourths**
**1/2 can pitted green-ripe
olives, cut into fourths**
1 small can pimientos, cubed
Sprinkle on:
1 teaspoon meat herb blend*
Pour around sides of pan so as
not to disturb olive mixture:
1/4 cup dry white wine
Cover tightly and bake at 375°
until done, about 1 hour.
Drain off liquid and skim off
excess fat. Thicken liquid with:
**2 tablespoons flour,
dissolved in a little water**
Add to thickened gravy:
**olives from pan and
1/2 can pitted ripe olives,
sliced into fourths**
**1/2 can pitted green-ripe
olives, sliced into fourths**
Spoon gravy over
chicken servings.
Serves 6

CHICKEN BOMBAY

Heat in large frying pan:
4 tablespoons butter
Add and fry until light brown:
**4 chickens, cut up into
serving pieces**
Cook until clear:
2 onions, minced
2 cloves garlic, minced in
2 tablespoons butter
Add, and continue to cook until
mushy, on very low heat:
4 tablespoons curry powder
Add and cook slowly for
15 minutes:
1/2 cup fresh coconut milk
Add and reheat:
3/4 cup sour cream
1/4 cup orange marmalade
**4 vegetable cubes,
or chicken cubes**

Dip fried chicken in this curry
mixture and lay in baking pan.
Add to remaining curry mixture:
2 cups chicken or turkey stock
Add to remaining butter in
chicken frying pan, and fry
until light brown:
1/2 cup coarse grated coconut
Add curry mixture to browned
coconut and mix together well.
Pour over the chicken in
baking pan.

Slice thin and then cut in half:
2 lemons or limes
Lay these on pieces of chicken
in pan. Cover tightly and bake
at 400° for about 45 minutes
or until done. Drain off juice
and thicken it slightly. Serve
with pieces of the baked lemon
on each portion, using juice.
Serves 8 or 10

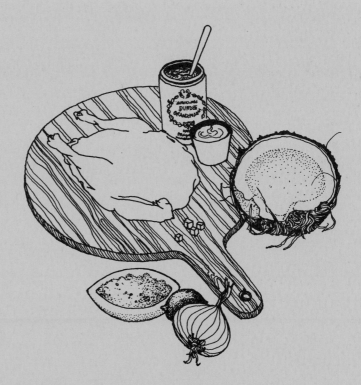

chicken

CHICKEN ALOHA

Melt in a saucepan that can be
later heated over water:
1/4 pound butter
Add and braise 5 minutes:
1 clove garlic, minced
4 green onions and tops, cut up
4 ounces fresh mushrooms, sliced
Add and mix well:
3 tablespoons flour
1 teaspoon salt
Add, cook and stir until thick:
1 cup Chablis or any white wine
1 tablespoon lemon juice
Add and heat over water:
1/3 cup canned bamboo shoots,
sliced
1/3 cup canned water
chestnuts, sliced
1 cup canned pineapple bits, drained
1/2 cup juice from
canned pineapple
1/4 cup blanched almonds,
toasted lightly
1 tablespoon frozen
orange-juice concentrate
1-1/2 tablespoons honey
When hot, add and mix gently:
1-1/2 pounds cooked chicken, diced
and salted with herb salt*
Serve over rice, garnished with:
macademia nuts
Serves 6

CHICKEN VERMOUTH

Nancy Adams, our hostess at the Ranch House, gave me this recipe and told me a little story about it which I shall pass along for those who may feel some hesitation about entering the world of gourmet cookery. "Sometimes, psychologically speaking," Nancy said, "we take a giant step in life. My mother was a fabulous cook; my sister, apparently with the greatest ease, became a fabulous cook. I observed all this with awe, helped set the table, entertained our guests, enjoyed the delicious food—and was secretly frightened at the thought of trying to understand all those kitchen mysteries. I thought good food must come from complicated recipes and take great skill to concoct. I felt I just wasn't that intelligent. Cooking wasn't my thing; if I tried, it could only end in disaster."

Nancy came West and went to visit a family friend in San Francisco. The friend took her sightseeing and shopping and about five o'clock in the afternoon they stopped at a market to get food for dinner, including a chicken. At home, her hostess spent a few minutes in the kitchen; then they had a drink and a little before six the husband came home. They had another drink and her friend went to the kitchen for another half hour or so.

"In no time at all after that," said Nancy, "we sat down to a dinner that tasted as though she had spent all day in the kitchen. If food that good could be that easily prepared, perhaps even I could cook. I asked for the recipe, tried it and it was a success. I had taken my giant step, and have been cooking like mad ever since."

Rub:
pieces of chicken
with garlic
Sprinkle with:
fresh lime juice
Let stand for at least 1/2 hour.
Dip chicken pieces in:
melted butter
Put pieces in baking pan and sprinkle with:
herb salt*
Add to melted butter and pour over chicken:
1/2 cup dry vermouth
(for 1 chicken)
Bake 1 hour at 350°, turning and basting every 15 minutes. Brown under broiler for a few minutes before serving.

chicken

CHICKEN CURAÇAO

Have the butcher quarter:
4 chickens
Brush chicken pieces
lightly with:
melted butter
Broil until golden brown, then
place in tightly covered baking
pan and bake at 400° until
tender, about 30 minutes.

To make sauce, mix together:
1 cup orange juice
1 teaspoon minced orange rind
Cut off rind very thin, using
none of the white part
1 cup white Karo
1/4 teaspoon cardamon, powdered
1 tablespoon butter
2 tablespoons brown sugar
1 tablespoon cornstarch,
dissolved in a little water
Cook until thickened, then
add and boil gently for 5 minutes:
1 orange, scrubbed and
sliced into 8 slices
When done add:
1/3 cup curaçao

Remove orange slices and put
aside to garnish chicken. Brush
chicken pieces again lightly
with melted butter and put under
broiler until they sizzle, then
plunge them in very hot sauce for
about 10 minutes. Use an orange
slice for each serving.
Serves 8

CHICKEN PAPRIKASH

Cut into serving pieces:
1 chicken
Mix together:
1/2 cup white flour
1 teaspoon paprika
1/2 teaspoon salt
1/4 teaspoon white pepper
Put the flour mixture into a paper
bag and shake the chicken pieces,
a few at a time, to coat them.

Melt in a skillet:
2 tablespoons butter
Brown chicken pieces in the
butter and remove them.

Add to skillet and cook 3 minutes:
1 onion, minced
2 tablespoons butter
Put chicken back in pan and add:
1 tablespoon paprika
1/2 cup water,
poured around, not over the
chicken. Cover and cook for
45 minutes. Turn the chicken
pieces as necessary to keep them
from sticking. If needed, add a
small amount of warm water. Remove
chicken when done and add to
pan gravy, mixing well:
2 tablespoons flour
When gravy is smooth, add:
2 cups sour cream
Cook gently until thick then add
chicken pieces and simmer slowly
for another 5 minutes to blend
flavors. Serve with rice or
peasant noodles.
Serves 4

CHICKEN HUNGARIAN

Cut into serving pieces:
4 chickens
Mix together:
1 cup white flour
2 teaspoons salt
1 teaspoon black pepper
4 teaspoons paprika
Coat chicken pieces with flour mixture and fry to golden red-brown in:
half butter, half olive oil
Place chicken pieces in pan with tight cover. Prepare the following sauce:

Sauté until nearly done:
4 tablespoons olive oil
2 cloves garlic, minced
1 large onion, sliced thin
Add and cook for 3 minutes:
2 green peppers, chopped coarse
1/2 teaspoon basil
1 tablespoon cilantro
1 cup chicken stock
Spoon sauce over chicken. Pour around edges of pan:
1-1/2 cups red wine

Cover tightly and bake at 400° until done—about 45 minutes. Drain liquid from chicken and skim well, then stir in:
1 teaspoon paprika
1 teaspoon chicken base
2 tablespoons cornstarch mixed in a little water
When sauce is thick, add and stir in well:
1 cup sour cream
To serve, spoon sauce over chicken pieces and garnish with sour cream.
Serves 8

CHICKEN CALAVO

Combine in a saucepan:
4 tablespoons butter
4 tablespoons flour
1/2 teaspoon herb salt*
Add and stir over low heat until thick:
1-1/2 cups milk
1 cup cream or evaporated milk
Add and mix lightly:
1 tablespoon sherry
1 pound cooked chicken, diced large
1/2 teaspoon herb salt*
1/2 teaspoon salt
Cut lengthwise, pit and peel:
avocados to cover bottom of casserole
Lay avocado halves in casserole, pit side up, and spoon the chicken mixture over them. Sprinkle lightly with:
Cheddar cheese, grated
Bake at 400° until edges of sauce start to bubble. Do not overcook, as avocados tend to develop an acid taste when overcooked.
Serves 6

chicken

CHICKEN CACCIATORE

This is the second of the three attractive names of meat dishes I decided to add to our menu as we began to serve meat. I went about the concocting of the dish much as I had done with the stroganoff, and here is the recipe as we now serve it.

Cook until cleared:
1 large onion, chopped fine
2 cloves garlic, chopped fine in
2 tablespoons olive oil
Add and cook 30 minutes:
1 No. 2-1/2 can Italian-style (pear) tomatoes
1 teaspoon salt
dash black pepper
1 bay leaf
(discard when cooked)
2 sprigs thyme
1 sprig basil
2 sprigs oregano
pinch rosemary
pinch summer savory
1/2 cup sliced mushrooms
4 tablespoons tomato paste (optional)

Lower heat and mash tomatoes; simmer 4 hours, adding:
3 tablespoons dry Burgundy
Dust with flour and brown in olive oil:
4 frying chickens, jointed
Place chicken in Dutch oven-type cooker and add enough sauce to cover it. Do not use too much sauce, just enough for each piece. A few tablespoons water in bottom of cooker will prevent sticking. Simmer 45 minutes or until chicken is done. Serve with vermicelli or other type pasta, with grated Parmesan cheese. Serves 8

CHICKEN TETRAZZINI

Cook and strain:
1-3/4 cups chicken broth
1-1/2 cups celery, chopped fine
1/2 cup onion, chopped fine
1/2 cup parsley
1 sprig marjoram
1 sprig thyme
1 small bay leaf (discard (discard when cooked)

Sauté:
3/4 pound fresh mushrooms, cut coarse in
4 tablespoons butter
In top of large double boiler put:
1-1/2 cups of above strained broth
1-1/2 cups coffee cream or evaporated milk
Heat and thicken with:
3/8 cup flour, dissolved in a little water
2-1/4 teaspoons salt
1/4 teaspoon fresh-ground black pepper
1/4 teaspoon garlic salt
Add mushrooms and:
2-1/2 pounds diced cooked chicken
3 tablespoons sherry
Heat over water. Place in small casseroles over cooked noodles, spaghetti or other pasta, top with grated Parmesan cheese and bread crumbs, and brown slightly under broiler.
Serves 8

CANNELLONI
WITH CHICKEN

Prepare the chicken filling as you would for chicken tetrazzini except that the mushrooms are optional and usually omitted. Use less sherry; a thin sauce will run out of the noodles.
Now make the noodles as directed (page 182) rolling them out very thin into rectangles about four by seven inches. Drop them into boiling salted water until just done—not soft. Lay flat on a board and fill one end of the rectangle. Fold over to make long cylinders and place in shallow baking pan. Spoon some of the chicken sauce over them and top with a generous sprinkling of Parmesan cheese. Bake at about 350° until the sauce begins to bubble around the edges. Have enough sauce so that they will not dry out. A little dry white wine is sometimes added at the edge of the pan to moisten and heighten the flavor. Serve on hot plates.

chicken

CHICKEN ENCHILADAS WITH GUACAMOLE & SOUR CREAM

(When you are cooking chickens and do not need to use the necks, backs and wings, freeze these pieces to be used later to make this delicious dish.)
Boil for 30 minutes in a covered pan, using very little water:
necks, backs and wings
from 2 chickens
Drain broth and reserve for other uses.
Remove meat from bones and cut into small pieces.
Make and mix with the chicken:
1 cup rich cream sauce
or béchamel sauce (page 24)
Do not make the mixture mushy.
Put in blender and blend thoroughly:
2 peeled and halved avocados
1 cup sour cream
1 sprig cilantro
1/2 teaspoon herb salt*

Pour avocado mixture into shallow pan or bowl.
Heat so that they will bend easily:
8 tortillas (must be fresh)
Put the chicken mixture on each tortilla, roll it up, and dip it into the avocado sauce mixture. Lay the rolls in a pan and heat in the oven to serving temperature. Serve topped with sour cream.
Serves 4

CHICKEN VERDE

Cut into serving pieces:
2 chickens
Fry until lightly brown in:
half butter, half olive oil
Lay pieces in pan that can be tightly covered and sprinkle lightly with:
herb salt*
Mix together:
6 green onions, cut diagonally into 1-inch pieces
2 garlic cloves, chopped fine
1 green pepper, cut in long thin strips

1/4 cup chopped parsley
1 green chili, minced (canned will do)
1/4 teaspoon basil
1/4 teaspoon marjoram
1/2 teaspoon cilantro
Heat in frying pan until almost smoking:
1/4 cup olive oil
Add chopped vegetables to oil and cook until just tender but not quite done, then add:
1 teaspoon herb salt*
1 pound fresh, or 1 small can tomatillos
(Fresh tomatillos are nearly always available in a good Mexican market.) Mix vegetables together and spoon over chicken pieces. Cover tightly and bake at 400° until done, about 45 minutes.
Drain off liquid and skim fat. Thicken gravy slightly with flour and serve over chicken.
Serves 6

chicken

CHICKEN HELENE

In the late 'twenties, toward the end of that era, I was with a jazz band, playing in a night club outside of Milwaukee. Nowadays kitchens of night clubs seem to specialize in beef, but the famed specialty of this Milwaukee club was chicken—fried chicken and chicken livers. The chef was a slight, always tired-looking woman named Helene. Her chicken soup was also much in demand and she had another popular dish which she called gizzard stew. She let me have the recipes and I think you will enjoy them.

To prepare chickens for four (or any multiple of this), cut into serving pieces:
2 chickens
Put the pieces in a pot, just cover with water and boil until nearly but not quite done. Drain and refrigerate the chicken pieces until very cold. Reserve the broth for soup.

In a Dutch oven or heavy iron pot with a lid, heat to 375°:
half butter, half lard,
to a depth of 2 or 3 inches (deeper for more chicken)
Dip cold chicken pieces in:
French-frying batter, (page 181),
to which has been added:
1 extra egg
Put the chicken into the hot fat, cover and fry until golden brown. The butter will go into the batter for flavor and the lard will keep the butter from burning or browning the chicken too fast. The cover causes the chicken to steam so that it is done all the way through. If these directions are followed exactly, you will have fried chicken with a flavor you may never have tasted before.

GIZZARD STEW

Have your butcher reserve for you:
2 pounds chicken gizzards
1 pound hearts and necks
Put giblets into pressure cooker or large pot with:
2 cups water
1/2 teaspoon meat herb blend*

Cook at 15 pounds pressure for 30 minutes, or covered until tender if pot is used; then drain and reserve broth.
Into another pot put:
1 cup carrots, cut into 1-inch pieces
1 cup celery, cut very coarse
1 cup onions, cut coarse
1/4 cup parsley, chopped
1 cup potatoes, diced large
broth from gizzards
Cook vegetables until just done, add enough extra water to make a stew, then add and cook until thickened:
2 tablespoons flour
mixed in a little water
Add and mix well:
1/2 teaspoon lemon juice
gizzards that have been cut in half
Serve in a large tureen and ladle into bowls. The stew should be juicy to make it enjoyable. Boiled noodles mixed with cooked, sliced onions and plenty of butter can be served with this stew.
Serves 8

CHEF HELENE'S CHICKEN LIVERS ESPAGNOLE

Put into kettle that can be covered and cook until clear:
1/4 cup olive oil
2 cloves garlic, minced
Mix together and add to garlic:
4 stalks celery, cut coarse
2 onions, cut coarse
1/4 cup parsley, chopped fine
1/2 teaspoon basil
1/2 teaspoon marjoram
1/4 teaspoon thyme
1/4 teaspoon pepper
2 teaspoons herb salt*
When onions and celery are just done but not mushy, add and bring to boil:
1 No. 303 can tomatoes, mashed
3 pimientos, chopped
1 teaspoon lemon or lime juice
2 cups mushrooms, sliced

Bring to high heat in a skillet:
4 tablespoons chicken fat or butter
(The fat can be heated higher than the butter before burning.)
Add and stir until they are well braised:
2 pounds chicken livers
When livers are cooked to taste, add the sauce and mix in well. Keep warm on low heat until flavors blend, at least 10 minutes. Serve with saffron or turmeric rice (page 77) This makes a fine luncheon dish served with a tossed green salad.
Serves 8

chicken

CHICKEN LIVERS & MUSHROOMS

Wash thoroughly and take out
any small parts of gall bladder
to avoid bitterness:
**1 pound chicken livers with
skin intact (do not use frozen)**
Braise livers in:
**2 tablespoons butter or
chicken fat**
Add:
**4 ounces mushrooms, sliced
1/2 teaspoon herb salt***
1/4 teaspoon meat herb blend*
**4 tablespoons chicken stock
1 teaspoon chicken base or
concentrate
2 tablespoons Chablis or
other white wine**
Cover and cook 10 minutes.
Thicken liquid with:
**2 tablespoons flour,
mixed in a little water**
Add and stir gently:
1/2 teaspoon lemon juice
Serve in casserole over rice.
Serves 4

CHICKEN CURRY

Cook until clear:
**1 onion, minced very fine
2 cloves garlic, minced fine in
4 tablespoons butter**
Add and mix in well:
3-1/2 teaspoons curry powder
Simmer for at least 5 minutes
on very low heat—10 minutes is
even better.
Add and blend in well:
**2 chicken cubes
1/4 teaspoon salt**
Mix with a little water and
stir in well:
4 tablespoons flour
When thoroughly mixed,
add and cook until thickened:
2 cups milk
Add and stir in well:
**2 tablespoons lemon juice
3 tablespoons apricot jam
or currant jelly
1 tablespoon sherry**
Add and mix in gently:
**3 cups cooked, diced
chicken, sprinkled with
herb salt***
Reheat in double boiler.
Serve with saffron rice (page 77)
and chutney.
Serves 4

CHICKEN LIVERS WITH ALLSPICE

Braise until nearly done,
about 3 minutes:
**1 pound washed chicken livers
1 small onion, sliced very thin, in
2 tablespoons butter**
Add and continue to cook slowly
for about 10 minutes:
**1 cup chicken broth (or
1 chicken cube in 1 cup water)
1/2 teaspoon salt (salt to taste
only, if cube is used)
1/2 teaspoon allspice
1 teaspoon brown sugar
1/2 teaspoon lemon juice**
When done, add and cook only
until thick:
**1 tablespoon cornstarch
dissolved in a little water**
Serve over saffron rice (page 77)
or turmeric rice (page 77) in
casserole. Garnish with:
**minced parsley and
chopped pimientos**
Serves 4

chicken

CHICKEN, SHRIMP OR CRAB GUMBO

Put in large kettle with
tight lid and boil for
15 minutes:
1 cup water (or chicken stock)
1-1/2 cups celery, cut coarse
1 cup onions, cut coarse
1/4 cup parsley, chopped fine
1/2 teaspoon salt
1 tablespoon sugar
**1/4 teaspoon fresh-ground
black pepper**
(More can be used; in the South
it is made very hot.)
4 bay leaves
(discard when cooked)
4 chicken cubes

Add and boil for 5 minutes:
**1/2 of No. 2-1/2 can
tomatoes, mashed**
Add and cook to thicken:
**2-1/2 tablespoons cornstarch,
dissolved in a little water**
Add and reheat but do not boil:
**1 8-ounce can cut okra,
or 1 cup fresh, cooked okra**
**1-1/2 pounds cooked,
diced chicken or fish**
**1/4 pound cooked, diced ham
(very essential for flavor)**
Add and stir in gently,
sprinkling over the mixture
and stirring in quickly after

all other ingredients are
added and the mixture is
still hot:
1 tablespoon gumbo filé
Do not try to mix the gumbo
filé in water first, for it
will not dissolve in the
gumbo but will make a nasty
grey-green paste.
Serves 8

seafood

"Seeing is deceiving; it's eating that's believing."
—James Thurber

Fresh fish sautéed in sweet butter, with a dash of herb salt and a squeeze of lemon or lime juice, makes a dish fit for any food enthusiast. Of course this is not sufficient for all fish, but is deliciously adequate for filet of sole or the little perch or sunfish caught in the rivers of the Middle West. Other, larger fish need something to bring out their special good flavor. Wine and herbs, used in various combinations, will do this to perfection.

One of the best herbs to use with fish is tarragon. Another is fresh, chopped dill weed; its flavor, in combination with a dry white wine, brings something extraordinary to the dish. Sweet marjoram, basil, thyme and especially borage are excellent. Summer savory in moderation, lovage and chives are also good. If the fish tends to be dry, sauces can be used to help it along. The flavor of the fish itself may be excellent, as is fresh salmon, but unless combined with something to offset the dryness it will not be enjoyable.
Be careful in using the strong herbs like rosemary, savory and sage.

seafood

HALIBUT
AUX FINES HERBES

Place in a casserole:
**8 slices (about 4 pounds)
halibut**
To make marinade, pound
in mortar:
1 tablespoon herb salt*
4 sprigs fresh tarragon
4 sprigs fresh lemon thyme
4 small leaves borage
Add herb mixture to:
1 cup white wine
3 tablespoons lemon juice
Mix well; then pour over the
fish and marinate for at
least 30 minutes. Drain off
liquid and thicken slightly
over low heat with:
**1 tablespoon cornstarch
(dissolved in a little water)**
Add:
**3/4 cup fresh mushrooms,
chopped fine**
**4 ounces mild Cheddar
cheese, shredded**

Spread mixture over fish in
casserole and bake at 400°
for about 25 minutes or until
sauce begins to bubble evenly
at the edges. Garnish with:
**thinly sliced toasted
almonds, sautéed and
minced parsley**
Serves 8

HALIBUT ESCOFFIER

Break off bottom part
and clean tops of:
18 asparagus spears
Stand asparagus in a tall
vessel that can be tightly
covered, add 1 cup water and
steam until tender. Drain
off water.
Combine in a saucepan:
4 tablespoons butter
8 tablespoons flour
Add, cook and stir until
just thick:

1 cup whole milk
1 cup coffee cream
1 bay leaf
(discard when cooked)
Mix together:
3 tablespoons white wine
1-1/2 teaspoons lemon juice
1/2 teaspoon herb salt*
Add and mix into wine:
2 cups fresh mushrooms, sliced
Cover and heat just to boiling
point then simmer for 3 minutes.
Add mushroom mixture to sauce
and stir in well.
Place in a casserole:
6 servings of halibut filet
Sprinkle lightly with:
herb salt*
Spoon the mushroom sauce over
the halibut, then lay on each
serving 3 asparagus spears.
Bake at 400° until the
sauce begins to bubble. Serve
immediately accompanied by
a tossed green salad and fresh,
cooked vegetables.
Serves 6

HALIBUT IN SOUR CREAM WITH DILL

Pound in mortar:
2 tablespoons fresh dill, chopped fine
1 leaf costmary, minced
1 leaf French sorrel
1 small sprig lemon thyme, chopped
1 teaspoon herb salt*
Mix ground herbs into:
1 cup sour cream
Place in buttered casserole:
4 halibut filets
Add sour cream sauce and bake at 400° until just bubbling. Serve immediately, topping each portion with a sprig of dill. Provide lemon wedges for extra tartness if desired.
Serves 4

seafood

POACHED SALMON WITH CAPER SAUCE

Lay in baking dish:
6 fresh salmon slices,
1-inch thick
Sprinkle with:
herb salt*
Pour around salmon, (but
do not quite cover it):
white wine
Cover baking dish with wax
paper. Do not use foil.
Poach at 400° for about
8 minutes or until wine is
bubbling well. Remove from
oven. Discard juice.

To make sauce, mix well
together:
1-1/2 cups béchamel sauce
(page 24)
1/2 cup capers
1/2 cup coffee cream
1/2 teaspoon herb salt*
2 tablespoons dry sauterne
Put salmon in casserole and
spoon caper sauce over it.
Bake at 400° until
sauce bubbles.
Serves 6

POACHED SALMON WITH RED WINE & MUSHROOMS

Lay in baking dish:
8 fresh salmon slices,
about 1-inch thick
Dot with:
butter
Squeeze over salmon:
lemon juice
Broil salmon until it
begins to brown a little.
Remove and keep warm.

Braise in a little butter:
2 green onions, chopped fine
2 shallots, chopped fine
2 stalks celery, chopped fine
2 ounces fresh mushrooms,
sliced thin
Pound in mortar, then add
to above and mix well:
2 sprigs marjoram
2 sprigs lemon thyme
2 leaves costmary or
1/2 leaf mint
1/2 teaspoon herb salt*
Cover salmon with this mixture,
then pour around it but do
not quite cover:
red wine

Cover dish with wax paper,
fitting paper tightly. Do not
use foil. Bake about 10 minutes
at 400°, or until done.
Remove paper and drain juice.
To juice, add:
1/2 pound butter
Reheat juice to almost boiling.
Put in blender:
2 egg yolks at room temperature
Start blender and add quickly
salmon juice and butter
while bubbling hot and:
dash of herb salt*
Blend about 15 seconds—no longer.
Serve over warm poached salmon,
garnished with parsley. .
Serves 8

BROILED SALMON
WITH SAUCE ALSACE

Slice thin:
2/3 cup fresh mushrooms
Butter lightly a very heavy
iron skillet. (A thin one will
cause the fish to dry out
during broiling.)
Lay close together in pan:
6 slices salmon, 1 - 1-1/4
inches thick, lightly salted
Broil salmon on first side
for 7 minutes.
While salmon is broiling,
put in blender and
whirl for 2 minutes:
1/2 tablespoon celery seeds
1/2 tablespoon poppy seeds
1/2 tablespoon sesame seeds
3/4 teaspoon onion salt
1/8 teaspoon peppercorns
3 gratings of fresh nutmeg
Melt and add to mixture in
blender and run for 1/2 minute:
1/2 pound butter, melted

Turn the slices of salmon
gently so as not to break them.
They have two long ends
extending from the belly of
the fish. Put into the belly
cavity of each salmon slice,
1/6 of the sliced mushrooms
and wrap the long ends around
them, making a small oasis of
mushrooms in the steak. Squeeze
over the salmon:
a few drops lemon juice
Salt lightly with:
herb salt*
Spoon sauce over salmon steaks
and broil second side for
3 minutes. Serve immediately.
Serves 6

seafood

FILET OF SOLE BÉARNAISE

Season filets of sole to taste with herb salt* and brown lightly on both sides in butter. Do not overcook the sole. Spoon béarnaise sauce (page 25) over the sole and serve immediately.

FILET OF SOLE AU GRATIN

Place filets of sole in casserole (halibut is also good). Spoon mornay sauce (page 24) over the sole and bake for 10 to 15 minutes at 400° until the sauce bubbles well at the edges.
Serve immediately.

FISKEPUDDING (FISH MOUSSE)

This dish makes a great first course for a large dinner. If possible, bake the mousse in a fish mold which can be obtained in gourmet and gift shops.

Put into blender:
**1 pound filet of sole
(or any tender white fish)
2 cups coffee cream
1/4 cup dry vermouth
1/4 teaspoon nutmeg
1 tablespoon herb salt***
**2 teaspoons lemon or lime juice
4 eggs**
Run until well mixed, at least 2 minutes, then add and continue mixing:
3 tablespoons potato starch
(cornstarch will not do)
Bake at 325° in greased pan or mold set in a shallow pan with 1 inch of boiling water in it, like a double boiler. Bake until pudding is firm in the middle, about 1 hour.

To prepare sauce for pudding, heat together gently:
**2 cups sour cream
1/2 teaspoon herb salt***
1 teaspoon fresh dill weed, chopped fine
After the pudding is baked, run a knife blade around the inside edge of the mould, place over the top of the mold a large platter which has been thoroughly warmed; then turn over the mold and platter.
The pudding will drop into it.
Serve the sauce in a bowl.
Serves 5 - 6

VARIATION:
SALMON FISKEPUDDING

For a fondue dinner party,
something light and tasty to
start the dinner was required.
My sister Dorothy had been
doing some food photography with
fresh salmon and had brought
us some that was leftover, which
we put in the freezer. Here was
a chance to experiment, so we
defrosted the salmon and used it
in place of the white fish. The
resulting mousse was a great
success, delicious and of
a wonderful pink color.

seafood

FILET OF SOLE MIMOSA

I was in Paris in the spring,
and I know why they call this
Sole Mimosa for it does look
like the flowering Mimosa
tree when served properly.
Sauté:
2 shallots, chopped fine in
2 tablespoons butter
Add and simmer for 5 minutes:
4 tablespoons cooked veal,
minced
4 mushrooms, chopped fine
4 sprigs parsley
4 sprigs marjoram
2 sprigs thyme
1 leaf costmary (optional)
Add and simmer again
for 5 minutes:
2 cups chicken stock
1/4 cup Chablis or other
white wine
1/2 teaspoon herb salt*
1/2 teaspoon lemon juice

Thicken with:
4 tablespoons flour
mixed in a little water
Fry in butter until just
done; do not overcook:
3 pounds filet of sole,
very fresh
Sprinkle lightly with:
herb salt*
Lay cooked sole on hot
platter and spoon sauce over it.
Garnish as follows.
Hardboil:
3 eggs
Separate and put through
a sieve the whites and yolks of
the eggs and (here is the
mimosa touch) sprinkle in
alternate rows of white and
yellow over the fish.
Serves 6

SOLE STUFFED
WITH BABY SHRIMP

Have ready:
4 pounds filet of Petrale sole
Sauté:
3 shallots, chopped fine in
3 tablespoons chicken fat
Add and simmer gently
for 5 minutes:
1 tablespoon minced ham
4 mushrooms, chopped fine
4 sprigs parsley, chopped fine
1/4 teaspoon fish herb blend*
Mix together and add:
1/2 cup Chablis
1/2 teaspoon herb salt*
2 envelopes, George Washington
golden seasoning (available
in most markets)
2 cups béchamel sauce (page 24)
Add and simmer again for
5 minutes:
4 cups cooked cocktail shrimp
Spread this mixture on the
sole filets, roll them up and
place them in a casserole.
Spoon over rolls:
2 cups mornay sauce (page 24)
Bake at 400° until sauce
begins to bubble.
Serves 8

FILET OF SOLE
FLORENTINE

Chop very fine:
1 10-ounce package frozen or
2 bunches raw spinach
Cook in very little water
for 1 minute. Drain and add:
1 teaspoon herb salt*
Spread a light bed of the
cooked spinach in a casserole
and place on top of it:
8 servings filet of sole
Mix together and spread
over the sole:
1-1/2 cups béchamel sauce
(page 24)
1-1/2 cups coffee cream
1-1/2 cups very sharp Cheddar
cheese, grated
1/2 teaspoon Worcestershire
sauce
dash herb salt*
dash cayenne pepper
2 teaspoons sherry
Bake at 400° until the sauce
begins to bubble around the
edges. Remove, garnish and
serve immediately.
Serves 8

SOLE VERONIQUE

Combine in a saucepan:
4 tablespoons butter
4 tablespoons flour
Add, cook and stir until
thick and smooth:
1 pint coffee cream
1/2 bay leaf
(discard when cooked)
1/2 teaspoon herb salt*
Add and mix in well:
1 beaten egg yolk
dash white pepper
2 teaspoons sherry
2 ounces small white
seedless grapes
Wash thoroughly:
2 pounds filet of sole
Lay filets in casserole and
sprinkle lightly with:
herb salt*
Spoon sauce over sole and
bake at 400° until sauce
begins to bubble. (If you
happen to have béchamel sauce
on hand you can use it in place
of the above sauce, adding the
wine and grapes.)
Garnish with:
parsley, chopped fine
lemon, sliced thin
paprika
Serves 6

seafood

CLAMS FLORENTINE

Drain and reserve juice from:
3 7-1/2-ounce cans minced clams
Cook until clear:
**3 green onions, minced fine, in
1/4 pound butter**
Mix together:
**3/4 cup white wine
clam juice**
Cook until reduced by one-half,
then add to cooked onions.

Cook 1 minute in covered
saucepan in very little
water (almost none):
3 bunches spinach, tops only
While spinach is cooking,
mix together:
**4 tablespoons cornstarch
mixed in a little water
1/2 cup whipping cream
1/2 teaspoon salt
1/4 teaspoon nutmeg**
Combine with clam-broth mixture
and cook until thickened; then
combine with clams.

Make a bed of the cooked spinach
in a casserole and sprinkle
it with:
herb salt*
Spoon on the clam mixture
and top with:
**1/2 cup grated Parmesan cheese
1/2 cup grated, aged Swiss cheese**
Bake at 400° for
15 minutes or until sauce
begins to bubble. Garnish with:
thin twisted slices of lemon
Serves 6

RED SNAPPER WITH HERBS

Braise lightly to set juices:
2 pounds filet of red snapper
4 tablespoons butter
Cook until tender:
1 small green onion,
chopped fine
1 tablespoon butter

Grind in mortar; then
add to cooked onion:
1 teaspoon herb salt*
2 small leaves
(or 1 large leaf) borage
2 sprigs marjoram
2 sprigs lemon thyme
3 leaves costmary
1 leaf lemon balm
2 sprigs tarragon
2 sprigs dill

Mix together and add to
herbs then cook until thick:
1 tablespoon lemon juice
2 tablespoons cornstarch
1 cup white wine
1 egg yolk
1 tablespoon sunflower seeds
(optional)
Place braised fish in buttered
casserole and pour sauce over it.
Bake at 400° only until sauce
bubbles. Do not overcook as
fish flakes easily. Garnish with
minced parsley and paprika.
Serves 4

RED SNAPPER
WITH BORAGE SAUCE

Place in baking pan:
6 servings (about 3 pounds)
red snapper filets
Sprinkle with:
1 large leaf borage, minced
1/2 teaspoon fish herb blend*
Cover with wax paper and bake
for 20 minutes at 350°.
Drain off juice and add, if
necessary, enough water to make
2/3 cup liquid.
Add to fish liquid and
bring to boil:
1/2 pound butter
Put liquid in warmed
blender with:
2 egg yolks
Whirl for 10 seconds, no more.
Put baked fish in attractive
casserole and pour sauce over it.
Reheat to serving temperature.
Raw pine nuts (pignolias) may
be added for texture.
Serves 6

seafood

CRAB VOISIN

This is a true story, and of all the incidents related in this book it is surely the most unusual. Inda and Jack Lynes, friends of my sister Dorothy, were up from Los Angeles one evening. Jack asked me if I would like to submit a recipe in a contest which was being arranged.

"If I should win, what would the prize be?" I asked.

"It's pretty fancy," he said, "an all-expense gourmet tour for you and your wife for two weeks, to London, Paris and Rome."

"I don't think I would be able to get away for that long right now. And if I won and could go, I'd probably eat myself to death—so I guess I must pass up the opportunity."

"Well, then, would you like to be one of the judges? Before you accept however, perhaps you should know more about the whole thing. Depending on how you feel, there may be a slight drawback . . . "

The contest was being sponsored by the Avocado Advisory Board, he told me, and invitations to submit recipes were sent by Earl MacAusland, editor of Gourmet Magazine, to well-known chefs all over the United States. Over three-hundred recipes had been submitted. There were to be three judges: an executive chef, an amateur chef, and someone who writes about food.

"You've just published a cookbook, so you qualify," Jack said, and continued: "The first two judges have been selected. The executive chef will be Hans Prager of Lawrey's Foods. The amateur chef is Sebastian Cabot of TV and film fame. For the third judge Lucius Beebe had been chosen, but he died. Then," Jack went on slowly, "we asked Art Ryon who wrote the dining-out column for the Los Angeles Times. He died."

"Wow!" I said, "I see what you mean—but I'm not superstitious. I'll be the third man."

The contest was to be judged in the executive suite of TWA in Los Angeles. The night before I was to go there I was sitting in my room reading the newspaper. Suddenly, I began to feel very ill, so much so I had to lie down on the bed. Of course I thought about the third-man superstition, but I told myself it was absolutely ridiculous. Eventually the illness passed and I was all right. The next morning, just so I wouldn't get bored, I asked a friend to go to Los Angeles with me. And I drove very, very carefully . . . There were quite a few people gathered about and cameras clicking as we did the judging and we finally agreed on one dish made with crab and avocado. The number on the dish identified it as the entry of Hippolyte Haultcouer, executive chef of the Voisin Restaurant in New York. He was called and told that he was the winner of the contest.

It was some time before I saw Jack and Inda again. My first question of course was:

"How did Hippolyte and his wife enjoy their trip?"

"They didn't go."

"Didn't go! Why not?"

"Because," Jack said, "he died."

Here is the winning recipe.
I have changed it a little
to suit our restaurant.

Prepare the following
rich cream sauce.
Combine in a saucepan:
3 tablespoons butter
3 tablespoons flour
Add and cook until thick:
1-1/4 cups coffee cream
1 bay leaf
(discard when cooked)
1/2 teaspoon herb salt*
When thick, add and
mix in well:
1 egg yolk
dash white pepper
To one half of the cream sauce
add and mix together well:
1 cup cooked crab meat, flaked
1 cup cooked rice
2 tablespoons pignolia
nuts, raw

Halve and peel:
4 avocados
Put the avocado halves in
a casserole and fill each half
with the crab mixture,
heaping it up.
Put the other half of the cream
sauce in a double boiler. Add
and mix in well:
1/3 cup aged sharp Cheddar
cheese, shredded
1-1/2 tablespoons coffee cream
1-1/2 tablespoons sherry
Cook until cheese is melted
then spoon sauce over avocados.
Bake at 400° only until
sauce starts to bubble. Do not
overcook, as avocados will then
develop an acid taste. They
should only be heated through.
This is a very rich dish so
allow only one half of an
avocado per person.
Serves 8

seafood

CRAB SALAD

For a wedding party of two
hundred, which we catered, the
pièce de résistance was
a huge man-eating clam shell
filled with this salad.
It made quite a show.

Mix together:
**1 pound crab meat,
cooked and flaked
1 cup celery, chopped fine
1/2 green pepper, chopped fine
1/2 cup cucumber, peeled
and chopped fine
1/2 cup green peas,
cooked and chilled
1/2 cup baby lima beans,
cooked and chilled
1 hard-boiled egg, sliced**

Add, sprinkling on as ingredients
are mixed, so it will be
evenly distributed:
1-1/2 teaspoons herb salt*
Mix together and add:
**1 cup mayonnaise
1 teaspoon lemon or lime juice**
Line the bowl in which
the salad is to be served with:
bronze lettuce leaves
Mound the crab mixture in
the bowl and garnish with:
blueberries, fresh or frozen
Scatter the berries over the
salad or make a design with
them. Chill the salad for at
least 4 hours before
serving. It should be served
very cold.
Serves 6

MUSHROOMS STUFFED WITH CRAB

Mix together thoroughly:
**1 pound crab meat, shredded
1/2 cup Monterey jack cheese,
shredded
1 egg white, beaten lightly
1 tablespoon white wine
1/2 teaspoon herb salt***
dash cayenne pepper
Combine and add, mixing in
thoroughly:
**1 cup soft white bread crumbs
1/2 cup rich white sauce
(page 24)**
Clean and remove stems from:
18 very large mushrooms
Place mushrooms right side up
in well-buttered skillet,
cover tightly and cook over
low heat until they are just
slightly soft to the touch.
Turn the mushrooms over and
salt them lightly with:
herb salt*
Using a small scoop to shape it,
put a scoop of the stuffing on
each mushroom and top with
a small amount of:
Monterey jack cheese
Bake at 400° until the
mushrooms begin to simmer.

Have ready:
**rounds of white toast, well
buttered**
Place mushrooms on toast.
Serve immediately, 3 to
a serving.
Serves 6
(If your guests feel at home
enough to call for seconds,
perhaps you had better have
extras ready!)

seafood

SCAMPI ALASSIO

This dish takes some time to prepare but it is so good I think you will find it worth the extra effort. It was first served to me in a waterfront restaurant in Alassio, Italy. The restaurant itself is old and the building dates from the twelfth century. Because it is on the waterfront all of the ironwork— hinges, rods, fasteners and such are weathered and rust pitted and have the wonderful patina of great age. At one end of the room are tables made of the coarsest heavy wood. No dividing wall separates the dining area from the kitchen at the other end of the room. You can watch the chef prepare the food. In the middle of his work area is a great chopping block such as one sees in butcher shops, and at one side in a brick wall is a fireplace where much of the food is cooked.

Cook for 3 minutes only in
boiling water:
32 large shrimp
2 bay leaves
Overcooking will toughen the
shrimp. Discard bay leaves;
shell and devein the shrimp.
Mix together and cook until
done but not mushy:
1/4 cup olive oil
1 stalk celery, chopped very fine
1 green pepper, chopped very fine
1 small carrot, chopped very fine
3 green onions, chopped very fine
1/4 teaspoon fish herb blend*
1/4 teaspoon herb salt*

Combine in another pan:
3 tablespoons butter
3 tablespoons flour
Add; then cook and stir
until thick:
1/2 cup milk
1/4 cup coffee cream
a small piece of bay leaf
(discard when cooked)
Add to cooked sauce:
3/4 cup cooked and flaked
crabmeat
Combine vegetables and sauce
and spread on a bed of:
cooked rice
Keep warm.

Put into a small frying pan
and cook for 1/2 minute:
2 cloves garlic, minced fine in
2 tablespoons olive oil
Remove and discard the garlic.
Put the boiled shrimp in the oil
and cook until heated through,
then add:
1/4 cup brandy
Flame the shrimp by heating the
brandy and then tipping the pan
until the alcohol catches fire.
When the flames die down, lay
the shrimp on top of the
vegetable and crab mixture and
pour the juice from the pan
over the entire dish.
Serves 4

SHRIMP CREOLE

Cook in pressure cooker
without cap, or until just done
but not mushy:
1 green pepper, cut coarse
1 clove garlic, minced
1 large onion, about 1 cup,
cut very coarse
1 cup celery, cut coarse
2 bay leaves
(discard when cooked)
1/2 cup chopped parsley
1/4 teaspoon thyme
dash cayenne pepper
When done, add:
1/3 cup tomato paste
1 teaspoon salt
Reheat and adjust seasoning
with salt.

Fry until clear:
2 cloves garlic, minced, in
4 tablespoons olive oil
Add and cook only enough to
thoroughly heat through:
1 pound cooked, peeled and
deveined shrimp, seasoned with
1/2 teaspoon herb salt*
2 turns from pepper mill
Mix shrimp with vegetable sauce.
Serve hot with rice.
Serves 8

seafood

CURRIED SHRIMP, INDIAN STYLE

Prepare a massala (spice mixture) by grinding in blender until fine (or pound in mortar):

1 tablespoon mustard seed
4 whole cloves
3/4 teaspoon poppy seeds
3/4 teaspoon peppercorns
1-1/2 teaspoons ground cardamon (or 5 whole seeds)
3/4 teaspoon turmeric powder

Cook until clear (about 2 minutes):

2 tablespoons butter
1/2 onion, minced fine
2 cloves garlic, minced

Add spice mixture and continue to cook very slowly until thick. Add and simmer for at least 15 minutes more:

1/2 cup coconut milk

Add and continue to cook until thoroughly heated, stirring frequently:

2-1/2 pounds cooked, peeled and deveined shrimp

Cook in pressure cooker for about 1 minute **without** the pressure cap (or in covered saucepan until tender but still crisp):

1/4 cup water
3 stalks celery, sliced coarse
2 onions, cut coarse
1 green pepper, cut coarse
(Vegetables should be in large pieces for texture.)

Mix the cooked, drained vegetables into the shrimp and massala mixture, and reheat over water. Do not allow to get too hot, as the shrimp will take on an unpleasant flavor if heated too much and too long. Add and continue to keep hot for about 15 minutes to blend flavors:

1/2 cup buttermilk
1/2 cup sour cream
1/2 teaspoon salt

Adjust seasoning with salt, and serve with saffron rice, chutney and other Indian condiments.
Serves 8

LOBSTER WITH LEMON THYME BUTTER

If you have an herb garden— and even a tiny one is a treasure beyond calculation— it should contain lemon thyme, which goes on year after year, so that it is always available.

Split:

2 lobsters, cooked and cleaned

Lay lobster in broiling pan and coat generously with the following butter sauce. Put in blender:

1/2 pound melted butter
1/2 teaspoon herb salt*
6 sprigs lemon thyme

Run until blended, about 1 minute. Broil coated lobster until it begins to brown slightly. Do not overcook as the lobster tends to dry out and toughen. Serve with:

drawn butter
lemon wedges
Serves 4

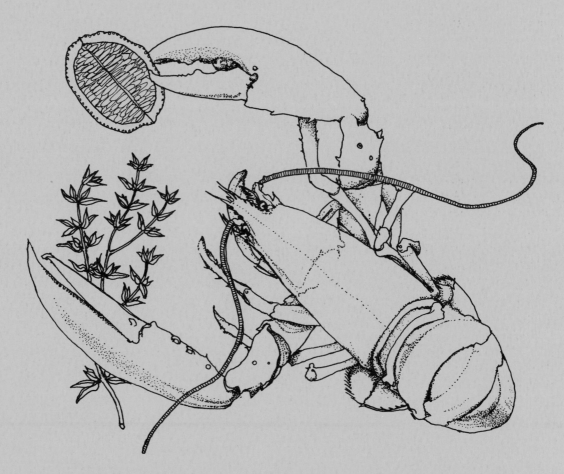

seafood

SCALLOPS ESPAGNOLE

Put into a pot that
can be covered:
1/4 cup olive oil
2 cloves garlic, minced
Cook until clear then add,
in the order named:
4 stalks celery, cut coarse
2 onions, cut coarse
2 green peppers, cut coarse
1/4 cup parsley, chopped fine
1/2 teaspoon basil
1/2 teaspoon marjoram
1/4 teaspoon thyme
1/4 teaspoon black pepper
2 sprigs cilantro, minced

Cook vegetables until just done
but not mushy; then add and
bring to boil:
1 No. 303 can tomatoes, mashed
3 pimientos, chopped
1 teaspoon lemon or lime juice
Prepare:
**turmeric or saffron rice
(page 77)**
Deep fry:
1 pound breaded scallops
Make a bed of rice in a casserole,
put the scallops on it and
pour the vegetable sauce over
them, heaping it in the center
so that the scallops show
around the edges.
Heat and serve.
Serves 4

SCALLOPS & CRAB
WITH SWEET HERBS

Mix together in a pan with
a cover:
1 pound scallops
1 tablespoon white wine
dash white pepper
1/2 bay leaf
(discard when cooked)
Grind together and add
to scallops:
1/4 teaspoon herb salt*
1 sprig thyme
1 sprig marjoram
1 shallot, minced
Simmer scallops very slowly
for 5 minutes.

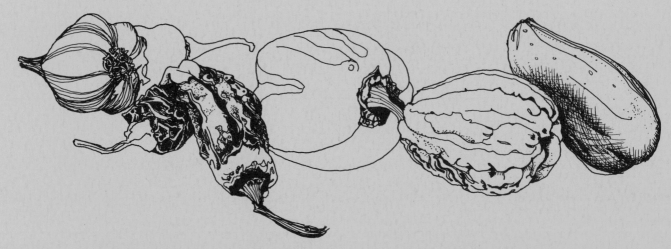

Cook for 2 minutes, gently:
2 cups sliced fresh mushrooms
1 tablespoon white wine
Combine in a saucepan:
3 tablespoons butter
3 tablespoons flour
Add, cook and stir until
thick:
1 cup milk
1 cup coffee cream
Add scallops and mushrooms
to sauce, then mix in:
1/2 pound cooked, shredded crab
Put mixture into casserole
and bake at 400° until sauce
begins to bubble, then top with:
mild, grated cheese
Place under broiler and
brown lightly.
Serves 6

SCALLOPS ST. JACQUES PROVENÇALE

Boil for 10 minutes,
peel and set aside:
2 eggs
Mix together:
1/4 cup white wine
1/4 cup water
1 small clove garlic,
minced very fine
1 shallot, chopped fine
1/4 teaspoon salt
1/8 teaspoon fresh-ground
black pepper
Add to mixture:
1 pound scallops
Simmer scallops gently for
about 5 minutes. Drain off
juice and reserve. If there
is more than 1 cup, boil to
reduce to that amount. If there
is less, add water to make 1 cup.
Add to juice:
1/4 cup whipping cream
1/4 teaspoon herb salt*
Combine:
2 tablespoons butter
2 tablespoons flour
Add to juice mixture, cook and
stir until thick, then add:
1 teaspoon lemon juice

Cut boiled eggs into quarters
lengthwise then once across
the center. Add scallops to
sauce, then gently
mix in the eggs.
Cook in tightly covered pan
until tender:
1 small carrot, shredded
1 small green pepper,
cut in thin strips
2 tablespoons butter
Put scallop mixture in casserole
and garnish with carrot and
green-pepper mixture.
Add in a decorative ring:
cherry tomatoes
Bake at 400° until sauce
begins to bubble.
Serve immediately.
Serves 4

lamb

Like veal, the best lamb is the youngest and therefore naturally tender. This is what is meant by spring lamb. If it isn't spring lamb it must be hung—that is, aged—for two or three weeks to tenderize it. You should make sure that your butcher is giving you aged lamb if it is not spring lamb. Older lamb that has been properly aged will be quite delicious; so, do not hesitate to question your butcher and don't be put off with a few words used to delude you.

In England and other parts of the Commonwealth, mutton, the older animal, is used much more frequently than it is in this country. It is handled quite differently than lamb; it is always a bit tough and so must be boiled or roasted a long time. It is important to know that by cooking you simply cannot make tough meat tender. You can cook it until it falls apart but the shreds will still be tough.

In this country, there is an old tradition of serving mint jelly with roast leg of lamb. At the Ranch House we try to avoid this cliché by serving chutney with the lamb and it is a happy companion to this distinctive meat. In the past, lamb was always roasted until it was well done and dull gray. This tradition is now disappearing. Lamb may be roasted or broiled to the pink stage, much like beef, if one likes it that way.

Because of its strong flavor, lamb needs a strong herb or spice to give it the proper accent. As a seasoning for lamb, black pepper is not nearly so necessary as it is with beef, but lamb surely must have a hearty dose of garlic. One of the best ways to season lamb, especially if you are marinating it, is to grind up the herbs to be used with herb salt or regular salt and plenty of fresh garlic. Through the garlic, the herbs will penetrate the meat. An excellent herb for lamb is the pungent rosemary; another is summer savory. Winter savory can be used sparingly—though I think it tends to impart the distinctive flavor of the hot dog whenever it is used.

ROAST PRIME RIB OF LAMB

Have your butcher cut in one
large piece, sawing the hinge
part just through for ease
in carving:
8 ribs of young lamb
Mix in blender, as marinade:
1 cup olive oil
2 cloves garlic, minced
1/4 teaspoon powdered thyme
**1/4 teaspoon powdered
summer savory**
1/2 teaspoon herb salt*
1/2 teaspoon rosemary
Rub marinade on sides and bottom
of ribs and put them in the
refrigerator in a covered pan to
marinate for at least 24 hours;
then remove from refrigerator
and let stand until ribs reach
room temperature. Roast at 350°
for 1 hour (less, if you want it
very pink) uncovered the last
15 minutes. Cut 2 ribs for each
serving. Garnish with:
fresh mint or sprigs of rosemary
Serves 4

STUFFED LEG OF LAMB

Have butcher bone,
and save the bones:
6-pound leg of lamb
Put into mixing bowl:
**2 cups cooked chicken,
minced**
gizzards and hearts can be used
2 cups prepared stuffing bread
Mix together and heat:
**2 cups chicken broth,
or 2 chicken cubes and water**
(If cubes are used salt
must be adjusted.)
1/4 teaspoon marjoram
1/4 teaspoon thyme
2 tablespoons orange juice
**3 tablespoons apricot jam or
orange marmalade**
2 sprigs parsley, chopped
1/4 teaspoon black pepper
**1 teaspoon salt (less
with cubes)**
Pour hot broth over stuffing.
Sprinkle boned lamb lightly
with:
herb salt*
Spoon stuffing into the lamb
cavity. Tie sides and ends
together loosely with string.
Lay lamb on piece of foil large
enough so that the sides will
come up around but not fold over
the lamb when it is put in
a baking pan. Put extra stuffing
around lamb. Bake at 350° for
1 hour or until done to taste.
It will be juicier if baked only
until pink but it must be cooked
enough to be tender.

Stew for 30 minutes:
**lamb bones in
2 cups water**
Take out bones and skim broth
well, then add to it:
any meat from bones
**1 tablespoon Italian sauce
(page 28)**
**1 tablespoon beef extract
(or 1 cube)**
Adjust sauce with:
salt
dash black pepper
Thicken with:
**1 tablespoon flour
dissolved in water**
Serve lamb sliced with a mound
of stuffing topped with sauce.
Chutney is a good garnish for
this dish.
Serves 10

lamb

LAMB DE MENTHE

Braise in fat cut from the lamb
until it is brown:
**2 pounds leg of lamb,
cut in 1-inch cubes**
Barely cover braised lamb with
hot water and cook until almost
tender, then add and cook until
vegetables are done but
not mushy:
**1 large carrot,
cut in 1/2-inch lengths
2 stalks celery,
cut in 1-inch pieces
1 green pepper, chopped coarse
1 teaspoon herb salt***
Add and keep warm:
**2 teaspoons green creme de menthe
1 cup peas**
Thicken juice with:
**1 tablespoon cornstarch
mixed in a little water**
Serve with green or red rice
(page 77)
Serves 4

HARICOT DES MOUTON

One of the last restaurants to
survive at Les Halles in Paris
is Monteil's. It used to be the
thing to do to go to the famed
old market after the theatre for
a bowl of onion soup; people in
full dress picked their way
among the vegetable crates to
find a place in the crowded
restaurants along with shoppers,
laborers and produce handlers.
Jean Claude Boulet at Monteil's
provided this recipe. It is still
served in the daytime to the
produce men. The market has been
moved to Rungis, near the Orly
airport; only remnants and
memories linger at Les Halles.

Soak overnight, then cook in
soaking water until tender:
**1/2 pound navy beans
1 onion, stuck with 2 cloves
1 carrot, sliced thin
salt and pepper to taste**
Remove onion and carrot
from beans.

Braise:
**3 pounds mutton, neck and
breast, cut into chunks, in
peanut oil**
Mix together and flour lightly:
**1 onion, chopped fine
1 carrot, chopped fine**
Add to mutton and cook for
1 hour:
**the floured, chopped vegetables
1 cup dry, white wine
1/2 cup water
1 tablespoon tomato paste
salt and pepper to taste
bouquet garni of:
    2 sprigs parsley
    1 sprig marjoram
    1 sprig thyme
    1 sprig basil**
Combine mutton and bean
mixtures. Discard herb bouquet.
Serve accompanied by a large
tossed salad.
Serves 6

143

lamb

LAMB ARMENIAN

I cannot take credit for thinking of the entree we call Lamb Armenian, but I do take credit for working out the final recipe. Jack Lynes, from the Lamb Institute suggested it. While dining at the Ranch House, he asked if we ever served lamb. I said we didn't because I knew of no interesting way to prepare it. I didn't want to serve the usual leg of lamb available in most restaurants. He thought awhile and then said: "Why not stuff eggplant with lamb?"

This jarred my imagination and the next day I started experimenting. After trying various cuts, I chose leg of lamb for its texture, moisture and flavor when combined with the eggplant. Lamb shoulder will not do. Here is the recipe as we now serve it:

Slice off the ends, about 3/4-inch from the stem of:
6 average-size eggplants
Reserve ends. Hollow out the eggplant, leaving the sides about 3/4-inch thick. Be careful not to puncture the sides, or the juice will run into the pan. Steam the eggplant in a large, covered kettle for 9 minutes, using very little water. Do not overcook. Remove and cool immediately, draining out any juice.
Fry until it begins to lose its red color. (It is not supposed to be completely cooked.):
3 pounds leg of lamb, ground
Add to cooked ground lamb and mix together well:
3 tablespoons fresh mint leaves, minced
(More mint can be used.)
1/4 cup cooked rice
1/4 cup old-fashioned oatmeal
1 cup Italian sauce (page 28)
2 teaspoons herb salt*
2 eggs
Stuff eggplants with this mixture. Put tops on eggplants and set them in a shallow pan. Bake at 400° uncovered for about 45 minutes.

Cook in pressure cooker for 30 minutes at 15 pounds or simmer in a kettle for several hours, adding more water as needed:
lamb bones
2 cups water
Skim off fat and remove bones.

Make sauce by heating in a saucepan:
2 cups lamb broth
(add more water, if necessary, to make 2 cups)
2 teaspoons beef extract (2 cubes)
1 tablespoon Italian sauce
Bring mixture to slow boil, then slowly stir in a paste of:
flour and water
Continue to stir over heat until the sauce is thickened, adding more flour and water if necessary.

Cut stuffed eggplant into halves and spoon sauce over each serving.
Serves 12

144

ARABIAN LAMB
& LENTILS

The dusky flavors of lamb and
lentils blend so well that
I experimented until I developed
a recipe that would incorporate
both. Here is a most hearty dish.

Cut into 1-inch cubes:
3 pounds lamb shoulder
(boned weight)
Braise lamb cubes until brown,
using any type of oil; then
combine with:
1/2 cup water
1 clove garlic, minced
1/2 teaspoon herb salt*
Cook in a pressure cooker
12 minutes at 15 pounds or
simmer in a heavy covered pan,
adding more water if necessary,
until the lamb is tender.

Combine in a pressure cooker
or pan:
1 cup lentils
2 cups liquid, using lamb
broth and water
2 celery stalks, chopped fine
1 onion, minced
2 garlic cloves, minced
1/2 teaspoon marjoram
1/4 teaspoon thyme
1/4 teaspoon rosemary
Cook at 15 pounds pressure for
14 minutes or simmer in a
covered pan until the lentils
are done.
Mix lamb and lentils together
and keep warm over very low
heat for at least 1/2 hour to
combine flavors. Reheat and
serve in small casseroles or
shallow bowls. Garnish with:
yogurt
The yogurt is essential and
more than a garnish, because
the tartness relieves the
heavy flavor of the lamb
and lentils.
Serves 8

lamb

TURLA QUOI
(LAMB RAGOUT)

A guest at the restaurant one evening was a dark-eyed, dark-skinned beauty. She wrote out this recipe for me—one of her favorite dishes, she said. Serve with Turkish coffee (page 183)
Sauté:
1 pound lamb, cubed and floured in
6 tablespoons olive oil
Put lamb into casserole that can be covered with:
2 green peppers, quartered
3 large tomatoes with seeds pressed out
2 cups string beans, cut across in half
1 small eggplant, peeled and cubed
2 carrots, cut in 1-inch pieces
1 large onion, cut into eighths
Mix together and stir in gently:
2 teaspoons salt
1 teaspoon black peppercorns
1 tablespoon paprika
1/4 teaspoon powdered cumin
Add just enough water to be seen through the top of the mixture. Bake at 375° for about 2 hours, covered.

This dish can be served as a casserole or can be mixed with lentils and served in small bowls. While the lamb and vegetables are baking, prepare lentils as follows:
2 cups washed lentils
4 cups water
2 large onions, sliced thin
2 teaspoons salt
1/2 teaspoon powdered coriander
1 bay leaf
(discard when cooked)
Cook very slowly until lentils are done; test after 1/2 hour (or cook in pressure cooker for 15 minutes at 15 pounds pressure).
Serves 6

PAT EATON'S MOUSSAKA

The wife of a long-time friend
of mine, who had lived in
Greece, gave me this wonderful
recipe that her Greek cook
used to make.
Stir into:
**2-1/2 cups béchamel sauce
(page 24)
2 egg yolks**
Brown in a frying pan:
**2 pounds ground lamb, in
4 tablespoons olive oil**
When brown, add and continue
to cook for about 15 minutes:
**1/4 teaspoon rosemary, chopped:
3 large onions, minced
3 tablespoons tomato paste
1/2 cup red wine
3 tablespoons parsley, chopped
1/4 teaspoon cinnamon
1/4 teaspoon salt
1/4 teaspoon black pepper
4 ounces mushrooms, sliced**
Cook the above until rather dry,
then mix into the béchamel
sauce.
Slice and broil until just done:
3 eggplants
Put a layer of the eggplant in
a baking dish. Sprinkle with:
**bread crumbs and
1/2 cup Parmesan cheese, grated**

Add a layer of the meat
mixture, another layer of
eggplant and so on, lightly
topping the casserole with the
grated cheese. Bake at 375°
for about 1 hour or until brown
on top. Cut into squares
and serve.
Serves 8

CURRIED LAMB

Braise in oil until brown:
2-1/2 pounds lamb, cubed
(leg of lamb is best)
Put browned lamb in pressure
cooker with 1/2 cup water and
cook for 10 minutes at
15 pounds pressure. (Or add 1 cup
water in a covered kettle
and simmer until tender.)
Drain and reserve juice.
(Leftover cooked lamb and lamb
gravy can be used instead of
the above.)
Cook until clear:
**2 cloves garlic, minced
1-1/2 cups onions, minced in
2 tablespoons butter**
Add and cook slowly for at least
5 minutes on very low heat:
2-1/2 tablespoons curry powder

Combine then mix well into
curry:
**1 cup juice from cooked lamb
(if necessary, add water to
make 1 cup)
1/2 cup fresh coconut milk
(or cow's milk)
2 tablespoons lemon juice
3 tablespoons apricot or
peach jam
1 teaspoon salt**
Thicken to good consistency
with:
**1-1/2 tablespoons cornstarch
mixed in a little water**

Steam in pressure cooker without
cap or in covered kettle until
just tender:
**1 cup carrots, cut coarse
1 cup celery, cut coarse
1 cup onions, cut coarse**
Salt to taste with:
herb salt*
Then add to sauce.
Combine and gently mix together:
**sauce and vegetable mixture
cooked lamb
1 cup uncooked peas, frozen**
Keep warm for at least
30 minutes before serving to
blend the flavors and thaw peas.
Serves 8

pork

Corn fed pork is not just a name or an advertising gimick. This type of grain is required to put the right kind of fat on the animal and the right flavor in the meat. Iowa pork is probably the best in the country because the farmers raise so much good corn there. The meat itself should be white, like prime veal, with a tender texture. If you have had pork chops that you could never cook tender, probably they were not corn-fed pork. So you must find a butcher who is interested in getting the finest pork obtainable.

In cooking pork, this warning cannot be overemphasized: The meat must be cooked well done. A parasite can be carried in the tissues of the pork called **trichina,** and its larvae can be passed along to humans with most serious and unpleasant results. If the pork is cooked until it is well done, there is no danger at all. Fortunately, pork is most delicious when it is most thoroughly cooked.

Pork is a sweet meat and it behaves well when a little brown or white sugar or syrup is added, as we use sweet sauces in baking hams. Therefore, herbs that have a sweetening effect go best with it, such as lemon verbena and pineapple sage; sweet marjoram and basil are also good in moderation, in combination with the first two and with some lovage added. Do not use strong herbs such as rosemary or winter savory, or even most summer savory. These are too overpowering. The exception is sage used in sausage, but that is a completely different treatment and taste.

PORK TENDERLOIN MUNICH

Cut into pieces that, when flattened with flat side of meat cleaver or large knife, will be about 2 inches in diameter:
**1 pork tenderloin
(4 - 5 pounds)**
Braise the slices in butter until done, very slowly at first, then with increasing heat; **they must not** be pink in the center.

To make sauce, sauté:
**4 tablespoons butter
2 green onions, including tops, minced
1 clove garlic, minced
1/2 cup celery tops, minced**
When done, stir in:
4 tablespoons flour

Add, cook and stir until thick:
**2 cups chicken broth
1 teaspoon basil
2 dashes nutmeg
2 teaspoons beef extract (2 cubes)
1/4 cup dry sauterne**
When thickened, add:
**1/2 cup coffee cream
1/2 cup sour cream**

To serve, spoon sauce over tenderloin pieces. A light sprinkling of Parmesan · cheese may also be added if desired. Crisp shoestring potatoes are an admirable companion to this dish; or potato pancakes can be the accompanying starch. Another suggestion is homemade boiled noodles tossed with fried bread crumbs and a bit of onion salt.
Serves 8

pork

**PORK CHOPS
WITH PINEAPPLE**

Fry in heavy iron skillet:
**pork chops with the tenderloin
left in
pineapple rings**
Sprinkle each side as they
cook with:
herb salt*
The juices of the pork should
give the pineapple a nice brown
color. Serve with steamed rice
and pour the pan juices over it.

150

PORK HAWAIIAN

Place in stainless-steel
pan, fitting in tightly to
cover bottom completely:
**8 center-cut pork chops,
cut 3/4-inch thick**
Season chops lightly with
salt, then spoon over them:
**8 tablespoons candied
ginger and syrup (powdered
ginger may be used,
sprinkled lightly)**
Place on each chop:
1 leaf pineapple sage
1 leaf lemon verbena
**fresh pineapple strips,
sliced thin**
Then sprinkle over each:
1 tablespoon brown sugar
Cover chops with:
**fresh or canned pineapple
juice, mixed with**
4 tablespoons vinegar
1/2 cup saki (optional)
Cover pan with foil and
bake at 400° for about
1 hour or until tender.
Pour off liquid and skim
off fat, then thicken
sauce with:
**cornstarch
dissolved in a little water**

Serve chops with thickened
sauce spooned over them.
Garnish with fresh coconut.
Minted rice is a very good
accompaniment to this dish.
Serves 8

PORK POLYNESIAN

Have butcher cut:
**6 pork chops, 1-1/2-inches thick
with tenderloin left in**
Ask the butcher to cut a
pocket in each chop, starting
at the small end, but without
cutting through so that the
stuffing will not leak.
Braise chops on each side in fat
after sprinkling them with:
herb salt*
Cook until clear and done:
1 small onion, chopped fine
1 clove garlic, minced in
2 tablespoons butter
Add and continue to cook
until smooth:
3/4 teaspoon curry powder

Mix together and add:
**1 No. 303 can fruit cocktail
and juice**
1-1/2 teaspoons lemon juice
Add, cook and stir until thick:
**2 teaspoons cornstarch
dissolved in very little water**
Using only the fruit, stuff each
pork chop and close the end
with toothpick. Lay chops in
baking pan and pour over them
the remaining juice mixed with:
1/4 cup pineapple juice
Sprinkle lightly with:
herb salt*
Cover pan with wax paper (don't
use foil as it will steam them
instead of baking them). Bake
at 350° for about 1 hour.
Drain off juice and thicken it
slightly with:
**1 teaspoon cornstarch
mixed in a little water**
For color, add:
red coloring, 1 or 2 drops only
Serve sauce over chops,
garnished with:
slices of fresh papaya
freshly grated coconut
macademia nuts, chopped
(optional, for glamour and
texture)

pork

PORK COINTREAU

So you want a special roast for
a special dinner? Well, here it is.
Have the butcher bone:
2 pork loins,
leaving in tenderloin
Then have him cut a strip
of the best
sirloin of beef
This strip should be the
same length as the pork
loin and about 1-inch thick
and 2-inches wide. Have him
tie the two loins together
with the pork inside,
making a long rolled roast.
The ties should be about
1-inch apart all along
the roast.

When you are ready to start
cooking the roast, stand
it on end and with the
handle of a wooden spoon
make four openings between
the segments of the roast.
Now mix together:
about 2/3 cup cointreau
1/2 teaspoon herb salt*
Spoon some of the cointreau
into each of the openings
in the roast, reserving
a few spoonfuls to brush
on the top and for basting.
Bake at 350° for about
1 hour and 15 minutes,
basting every 15 minutes
with the extra sauce and
the pan juices. The beef
should be pink when done.

Liquefy in blender:
1 No. 303 can fruit cocktail
3 tablespoons cointreau
1/4 teaspoon herb salt*
2 drops green coloring
9 drops red coloring
Bring mixture to boil in
saucepan and thicken with:
1 tablespoon cornstarch
dissolved in a little water
The sauce should be just
runny enough to be
attractive when spooned
over the slices of meat.
Keep the parts of the roast
together when slicing, for
eye appeal.

Broil in:
butter
slices of pineapple,
1 for each serving
Fill holes in pineapple with:
chopped walnuts
For each serving,
spear on a toothpick:
1 piece spiced cantaloupe
1 green cherry
1 red cherry
Stick the toothpicks in
the sliced pineapple, red
cherry on top, and with
a spatula put a pineapple
slice on each serving of
meat; or serve the roast
on a heated platter,
garnished with pineapple
slices. Between the
pineapple slices sprinkle:
coconut curls, heated
and lightly salted
All this makes a very
dramatic entree which will
bring exclamations from
your guests, and none of
it is a bit difficult to do!

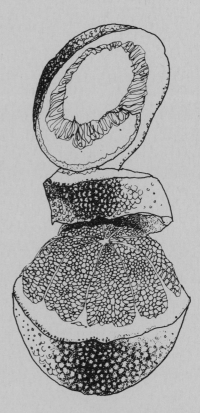

pork

GINGERED HAM AND ORANGES

Place in shallow baking pan:
**1 center-cut slice of ham,
1-inch thick**
Spread over ham:
**candied ginger and syrup,
to taste (not too much)
pickled onions, chopped
8 1/4-inch thick slices fresh
orange with skin on**
Spoon on each orange slice:
1 teaspoon orange marmalade
Bake at 400°, uncovered, for
about 45 minutes, longer will
tend to dry it out. When done,
remove ham and thicken sauce
in pan with:
**cornstarch
dissolved in a little water**
Spoon sauce over ham and garnish
with the baked orange slices.

BAKED HAM
WITH CURRIED FRUIT

Have butcher draw the bone from:
1 ham
(This makes it easier to slice.)
Bake ham according to directions
on package or from butcher. The
last hour of baking, baste the
ham with the following sauce.

Drain, reserving syrup:
1 No. 2-1/2 can each of peach,
pear and apricot halves
Combine 4 cups of the fruit
syrup with:
3/4 cup water
3 tablespoons lemon juice
2 tablespoons brown sugar
2 teaspoons curry powder
2 tablespoons cornstarch
dissolved in a little water
Cook and stir over low heat
until the sauce is thick.

Place the drained fruit in a
baking pan, pit side up, and
spoon on each piece of fruit the
following mixture which has been
heated until dissolved:
4 tablespoons butter, melted
1/2 cup brown sugar
2 tablespoons curry powder
Bake fruit for 15 minutes
at 325°. Serve with ham slices.
Turmeric rice makes an
excellent accompaniment.

PORK CHOPS IOWA STYLE

Braise on both sides in fat:
4 large, thick loin
chops with tenderloin left in
Salt on both sides with:
herb salt*
Lay braised chops in a
casserole that can be
tightly covered.

Mix together and
spread over chops:
1 No. 303 can cream-style
corn with liquid
1/2 green pepper,
chopped very fine
1 pimiento, chopped fine
2 tablespoons coffee
cream mixed with
1 tablespoon flour
1/2 teaspoon meat herb blend*
1/2 teaspoon herb salt*
Cover tightly and bake
at 350° for about 1 hour.
Remove chops and adjust thickness
of sauce by thinning with cream,
if too thick, or adding flour
and water paste over heat, if
too thin. Serve sauce over chops.
Mashed potatoes are almost
a must with this Midwestern dish
which was so much enjoyed by my
family on cold wintery nights.

veal

Several of these veal recipes come from Europe where I learned to prepare them with true veal, which is the meat of the young calf that has never fed on anything but its mother's milk. The meat is white and very tender and of a delicate and distinctive flavor. It needs barely any cooking and many people like to eat it accompanied only by a wedge of lemon to squeeze over it. In the dairy countries such as Denmark and Holland there is an ample supply of these small young animals, and white veal is plentiful everywhere in Europe.

White veal is rare in this country, especially in the Western states. It is less profitable to slaughter animals weighing under 400 pounds; this means that the calves have started to feed away from their mothers. The meat, therefore, begins to turn red and the texture changes from very soft to firm. Although we speak of this as veal, it is really only young beef which has already begun to take on the characteristic beef flavor. If you cannot find the white veal, you will need to cook the meat a little longer than the time given. When you can get white veal give it the gentlest treatment, and enjoy a special treat.

The herbs to use with veal should be the delicate ones like sweet marjoram, basil, and a little pinch of thyme, plus parsley. The addition of chopped lovage is acceptable. Never use a strong herb, especially with white veal—it will kill the flavor. Veal cooked in wine is an extraordinary combination. Imagine tender morsels pounded thin and gently simmered in a fine white Rhine wine.

VEAL ALLEGRO

Slice in thin slices:
**1 very young and tender
veal tip, 4 to 5 pounds**
Braise in:
butter
Season to taste with:
herb salt*
Place slices on hot platter
and spoon over them the
following sauce.

Braise:
**2 green onions, sliced, in
4 tablespoons butter**
Stir in:
4 tablespoons flour
Add and stir until thickened:
**1 pint coffee cream
2 teaspoons beef extract
(2 cubes)**

When thick, add:
**8 ounces mushrooms and stems,
sliced
2 apples, peeled, quartered,
cored and sliced following
the curve of the apples,
making nearly flat pieces**
Pound together in mortar
and add:
1/2 teaspoon herb salt*
**pinch each of basil, marjoram,
thyme, celery seed
1/2 teaspoon minced parsley**
Then add:
**4 tablespoons sherry
1/2 teaspoon lemon juice**
Simmer this sauce until apples
just begin to get tender.
Mushrooms and apple slices
should not be overcooked, but
cooked just until the raw taste
and texture have disappeared.
This is the most important part
of the entire preparation.
Serves 8

veal

VEAL FRANÇOIS

Cut into 1-inch cubes and
braise until well browned:
6 pounds veal in
1/4 pound butter
Put veal cubes into saucepan,
leaving butter in frying pan.
Add to veal cubes and cook
until just tender:
1/2 cup sherry
1/2 cup water
2 tablespoons chicken base
1/2 bay leaf
(discard when cooked)
Add to butter in frying pan:
1 pound mushrooms, sliced
1/2 teaspoon herb salt*
1 pint coffee cream
3 tablespoons flour
mixed in a little of the cream
When veal is tender add it to
the mushroom mixture and adjust
seasoning with:
salt
good dash of black pepper
Heat to serving temperature
and serve with rice. Older veal
can be used for this recipe.
Serves 8

VEAL HUNGARIAN

This is a very good dish for entertaining as it will not be spoiled if guests are late. Older veal can be used, but must be cooked longer.

Cut in 1-inch cubes and braise:
6 pounds veal shoulder (boned weight) in
1/4 pound butter
Add and cook 6 minutes:
1 cup water
4 cups onions, sliced
2 cups carrots, sliced
2 cups celery, sliced thin
4 cloves garlic, minced
4 bay leaves
(discard when cooked)
4 tablespoons paprika
2 cups chicken stock
4 tablespoons chicken base
Add and cook very slowly until veal is almost tender:
4 tablespoons tomato paste
4 tablespoons flour,
mixed with a little water
Add and cook until veal is completely tender:
2 cups green peppers, sliced
2 cups sliced sweet red peppers, if available
or 1 3-ounce can pimientos, chopped
Serve in individual casseroles over:
peasant noodles (page 182)
Garnish with:
dollop of sour cream
parsley, chopped
Serves 12 or more

VEAL MINNESOTA

Have butcher cut 1/2-inch thick strips into 2-inch pieces:
3 pounds veal tip
Pound veal into scallops and braise in:
4 tablespoons butter
Remove veal from frying pan and lay it in a shallow baking pan.
Braise in the butter from the veal:
1/2 cup mushrooms, sliced
Add to mushrooms:
1/2 cup sherry
2 cups chicken stock
1/2 teaspoon herb salt*
Grind in mortar and add to mushroom mixture:
1/2 teaspoon salt
1 large sprig basil
2 sprigs lemon thyme
1 large sprig lemon balm
2 leaves costmary
3 sprigs marjoram
1/2 teaspoon celery seeds
Wash and add to mixture:
1/2 cup wild rice
Pour mixture over veal, cover and bake for 1 hour at 400°.
Serve in individual casseroles.
Serves 6

veal

VEAL SCALOPPINI

Here is the third of those remembered names that became one of our menu standards when we started serving meat at the Ranch House. As with the other two, I first read recipes then put them aside and through experimentation and refinement arrived at this recipe:

Have butcher slice into strips, 1-1/2 x 3 inches, 1/4-inch thick:
1 veal tip, 4 or more pounds
Dip slices lightly in:
Parmesan cheese, grated
Brown quickly in butter in very hot skillet. Keep pan scraped and save scrapings.

Set browned veal aside and sauté in pan where it was browned, adding scrapings:
1-1/2 cups sliced mushrooms in 4 tablespoons butter
Add and bring to boil:
1 cup sherry

1/2 cup sauterne
1/2 cup Chablis
1/2 cup béchamel sauce (page 24)
1 teaspoon beef extract (1 cube)
1-1/2 teaspoons herb salt*
1/2 teaspoon savory herb blend*
1/2 cup water
dash cayenne or black pepper
Mix well in skillet and cook until well blended.
Lay the strips of veal in a baking pan and pour the sauce from the skillet over them. Bake tightly covered until tender, about 45 minutes to 1 hour, at 400°. Remove veal and thicken gravy with a little flour mixed in water. Serve in small casseroles.
Serves 8

VEAL PARISIENNE

Cut into strips 2 x 1/2-inch:
1 veal tip, 4 to 5 pounds
Pound strips into scallops; then sear quickly in butter in heavy iron skillet, keeping pan very hot so meat will not lose juice. Remove meat and pour into skillet:

sherry to a depth of 1/2-inch
1-1/4 cups sour cream, beaten to take out lumps
Scrape up fryings in skillet and stir mixture until smooth, then add:
2 tablespoons beef extract
1 cup water
fresh-ground black pepper
1 bay leaf
(discard when cooked)
Bring mixture to boil, then pour over veal scallops in baking dish. Cover tightly and bake for 1-1/2 hours or until done.

To make sauce, wash and drain:
4 ounces French sorrel, tops only
Cook tops 2 minutes in pan with:
2 tablespoons water
Put through sieve and add:
1-1/2 cups sour cream
1/2 teaspoon herb salt*
1 or 2 drops green coloring
Thicken sauce by cooking slightly; then pour over baked scallops in casserole, and serve.
Serves 8

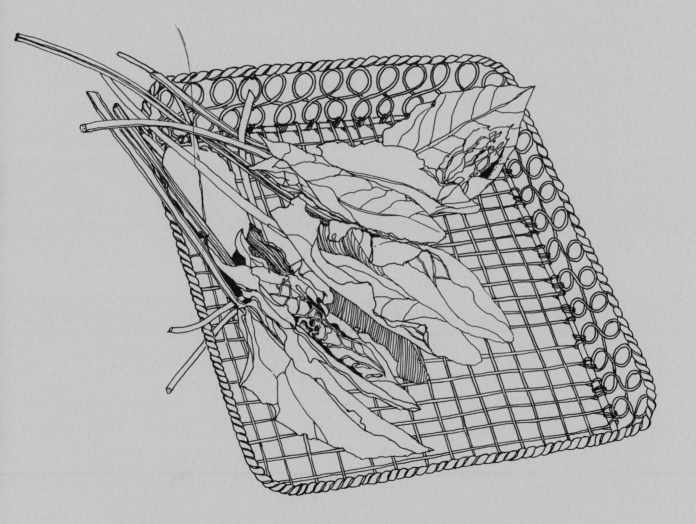

veal

PREPARATION OF SWEETBREADS

Wash the sweetbreads and squeeze all dark places free of blood; then soak them in cold water for at least 1 hour. Blanch the sweetbreads by boiling in water for 20 minutes. Drain them, and plunge them into cold water; then soak them another 30 minutes. Separate them into 1-1/2-inch pieces, removing any membranes and dark parts.

SWEETBREADS ALSACE

Sauté for about 10 minutes or until tender:
3 pounds prepared sweetbreads in
6 tablespoons butter
At the last minute or 2, add:
12 medium-sized mushrooms, sliced

Mix together:
1/2 cup sherry
3 teaspoons beef extract
1 teaspoon herb salt*
1/4 teaspoon white pepper
1 cup whipping cream
Mix together:
3 tablespoons flour
3 tablespoons butter
Add to sherry mixture, heat and stir until it thickens; then add and stir until smooth:
6 tablespoons sherry
6 tablespoons coffee cream
Mix sweetbreads and sauce together and serve in individual casseroles on:
thin slices of buttered toast
Serves 6

SWEETBREADS AU CRÈME

Prepare as directed then sauté for 20 minutes:
2 pounds sweetbreads in
6 tablespoons butter
At the last minute or 2 add:
1/2 pound large mushrooms, sliced

Heat to boiling point:
1 pint coffee cream
1/2 pint whipping cream
1 bay leaf
(discard when cooked)
Combine and stir into cream:
2 tablespoons butter
4 tablespoons flour
Add:
2 teaspoons beef extract
Pound in mortar and add:
1/2 teaspoon herb salt*
1 sprig marjoram
1 sprig basil
1/8 teaspoon white pepper
Cook and stir sauce until thick over low heat; then stir in well:
2 ounces sherry (or brandy)
Mix sauce with sweetbreads and serve with:
cooked rice
Garnish with:
parsley, minced
paprika
Serves 6

BROILED SWEETBREADS

Prepare as previously directed:
6 large, half sweetbreads
Broil them until nicely done
and tender, about 20 minutes,
not too near the grill to burn
them. Set aside and keep warm.
To make the sauce cook until
tender:
2 shallots, chopped
2 sprigs marjoram, chopped
2 sprigs basil, chopped in
1/2 pound butter
When just done, add and
and mix well:
1/2 cup parsley, minced fine
Put cooked sweetbreads on hot
platter and pour the sauce over
them. It should be slightly
brown.
Garnish with:
6 tablespoons bread crumbs,
lightly browned in
4 tablespoons butter
Serves 6

breads and spreads

NUT BREAD

Beat lightly in mixing bowl:
1 egg
Add, and beat with egg:
1-1/2 cups lukewarm milk
1 tablespoon melted butter
1 teaspoon vanilla
Sift together; then mix well into liquid:
4 cups sifted all-purpose white flour
1 cup sugar
1 teaspoon salt
1/4 teaspoon allspice
4 teaspoons Royal Baking powder
Add and mix well:
1 cup walnuts, coarsely chopped
Let stand for 15 minutes then bake at 325° for 1 hour in large greased loaf pan.
Cool on wire rack.

FRESH COCONUT-GINGER BREAD

Mix together in a pan:
1/2 cup warm water
2-1/4 cups fresh coconut milk
(The coconut milk can be made by running in the blender for 5 minutes 1 cup of hot water and 1/2 cup grated fresh coconut meat; then repeat, using the same portions; or it may be obtained frozen and completely defrosted before using.) Add to coconut milk and water:
1 tablespoon butter
1/3 cup honey
2 teaspoons salt
1 tablespoon fresh ginger root, grated (more if desired)
Heat to 90°, about body temperature, then add and stir in:
2 packages dry yeast
Let stand until yeast dissolves and little bubbles begin to appear; then add and mix in well, first with a spoon then by hand to get in all the flour:
6-2/3 cups sifted whole-wheat flour
1 cup grated fresh coconut
(Accurate measurements are important; 5-3/4 cups unsifted flour equals 6-2/3 cups sifted flour.) Knead until dough is thoroughly mixed. It should be moist and slightly sticky. Cover with a cloth and set in a warm place to rise to double its bulk. This will take 15 to 20 minutes. Turn out onto a floured board and knead again for at least 10 minutes, pressing the dough down flat, folding it over and turning it around until the large air bubbles are squeezed out. This will make a good texture. Dough should be springy to the touch, good and tough.
Cut the dough into 2 equal parts. Flatten each piece out and fold over. Repeat this flattening and folding until, when rolled up, each piece forms a log the size of the pan. Grease the pans with shortening; butter will burn and the bread will stick to the pan. When the dough is put into the pan be sure the upper part is smooth and unbroken; a break will make the dough break out in bubbles. Let rise until dough is about 1 inch higher than the rim of the pan. Bake at 375° for 45 minutes. Turn out on rack to cool.

breads and spreads

CALIFORNIA SPICE BREAD

Several years ago my friend
Martha Agnew mentioned that
sometime I should experiment with
a bread she called Pain des
Épices. I thought of it now and
then but never seemed to get
around to doing anything about it.
Then another friend, Torre
Taggart, returned from living
in India, bringing talk and
recipes from faraway lands. Now
was the time to try the spice
bread recipe. I have brought
the East and West together in
this recipe, adding soy flour
which is not generally used in
India. Here is the tested recipe
and I think the only difficulty
you will have will be to prevent
its being entirely consumed
before the loaf has a chance
to cool.

Sift before measuring:
3/4 cup soy flour
Mix with flour and heat to
lukewarm, about 90°:
1/4 cup wheat germ
2 teaspoons salt
1 tablespoon butter
1/4 cup honey
3/4 cup water
1 cup whole milk
Add to lukewarm mixture and stir
in well:
2 packages dry yeast
2 teaspoons powdered
cardamon seeds
2 teaspoons powdered
coriander seeds
1 teaspoon nutmeg
1/4 teaspoon allspice
Let stand at least 15 minutes so
that yeast can reconstitute,
making the mixture frothy. Then
with large spoon stir in:
2 cups white unbleached flour,
sifted before measuring
When this is well mixed in, add
and continue to mix:
2 cups white unbleached flour,
sifted before measuring
To get all of the flour mixed in
turn the dough out on a lightly

floured board and knead it.
Continue the kneading until the
dough is smooth and springy. Put
in a bowl to rise, smooth side
up, until double its bulk,
perhaps 30 minutes. Turn out on
the floured board and knead again
for another 10 minutes or so,
to give it a good texture. Divide
the dough in half and knead and
shape each piece into a log,
folding the ends under so that
the top will have a smooth
surface skin. There must be no
breaks in the top or the loaf
will burst open when baking. Put
the logs into small well-buttered
bread tins and let rise to about
1/2-inch above the rim of the pan.
Bake at 360° for 35 minutes.
When baked, remove from pans and
put on wire cooling rack or stand
on end, otherwise the surface of
the loaf will sweat and become
wet and soft. The top may be
brushed with butter but this is
not necessary.

BANANA-APRICOT NUT BREAD

Cream together:
1/3 cup butter (at room temperature)
2/3 cup sugar
Add and beat well:
2 eggs
Mix together:
1 cup sliced medium-ripe bananas
1/4 cup buttermilk
Sift together:
1-1/4 cups sifted flour
1/2 teaspoon salt
1 teaspoon Royal baking powder
1/2 teaspoon powdered cardamon
1/2 teaspoon baking soda
Add banana mixture and flour mixture alternately to egg mixture, then stir in:
1 cup whole bran
3/4 cup dried apricots, chopped
1/2 cup walnuts, chopped
Put into 9x5x3 greased pan and bake at 375° for 1 hour or until done. Cool on wire rack.

SURRULITOS DE MAIZ

Mix together:
1 cup cornmeal
1 teaspoon garlic salt
1 teaspoon sea salt (available at health food stores)
1 teaspoon cilantro, minced
1 tablespoon butter
1 teaspoon dehydrated vegetable broth (1 vegetable cube)
1-1/4 cups water
If the cornmeal is coarse, use a little less water.
Cook until mixture thickens, stirring constantly, then lower heat and cook for 15 to 20 minutes, stirring once or twice. Set aside to cool a little then mix in:
2 generous tablespoons grated Parmesan cheese
When the mush is cool enough to handle, put a heaping tablespoon in the palm of your hand and form it into a ball; then roll it between the palms to make the 'surrulito' about 2-inches long. In Puerto Rico these are fried, but they are most delicious baked. Put a small amount of oil on a cookie sheet and roll each surrulito in it as you arrange them on the sheet. Bake at 350° until they are brown on top, then turn them over. They can also be cooked under the broiler if watched carefully and broiled on both sides. They get deliciously brown and crisp. They can be frozen for future use.

breads and spreads

RANCH HOUSE
PATÉ WITH COGNAC

A ballerina, Carmeleta Maracci,
gave me this recipe. I have
modified it a little.
Braise only until clear, do
not brown:
**4 green onions, including tops,
chopped fine, in
4 tablespoons butter**
Add and cook for 10 minutes,
covered:
**1-1/2 pounds chicken livers
(turkey or goose livers may
be used)**
Mix together and add to livers:
**2 teaspoons salt
2 teaspoons dry mustard
1/2 teaspoon fresh ground
nutmeg
1/4 teaspoon ground cloves**
Run mixture in blender at high
speed for 2 minutes, then add
and run again, stirring at
least twice:
**1/4 pound butter
8 ounces Philadelphia
cream cheese
1/2 cup cognac**
You may also add:
truffles

They should be chopped and
added after the paté is
removed from the blender. Chill
for at least 24 hours before
serving. The paté can be put
into attractive little dishes,
garnished with a slice of truffle
and stored. There are those who
will consider the addition of the
cream cheese a sacrilege but it
smooths the paté so beautifully
that we disregard the purists.

FILLING FOR
DATE NUT BREAD

Whip in mixer for 2 minutes:
**4 ounces Philadelphia
cream cheese
3 tablespoons frozen orange
concentrate
1 tablespoon honey
1/16 teaspoon cardamon
seed, powdered**

PIMIENTO CHEESE SPREAD

Sometimes you need to make a lot of sandwiches quickly. Here is a recipe for 50 delicious sandwiches that can be made without fuss or bother.

Whip in mixer until light and fluffy:
1-1/2 pounds Philadelphia cream cheese
1-1/2 pounds butter, room temperature
1-1/2 teaspoons herb salt*
Add and whip 1/2 minute, just until incorporated:
3 7-ounce cans pimientos, chopped

MINCED CHICKEN FILLING

Mince:
2 cups cooked chicken
Salt lightly with:
herb salt*
Add, mix well and chill:
1/2 cup celery hearts and leaves, chopped
3/4 cup mayonnaise
1/4 cup sour cream
1/4 cup toasted, sliced almonds
As a variation, add 1 or both:
parsley, minced fine
pimientos, chopped fine

CURRIED EGG

Boil, cool and peel; then slice thin:
4 eggs
Mix together:
1/2 cup mayonnaise
1/2 teaspoon curry powder
2 teaspoons mustard (the type made with horseradish is best)
1/2 teaspoon herb salt*
1 teaspoon chutney, mashed fine
Mix with egg slices. This is good on any type of bread.

GREEN CRUNCH

Stir or whip until smooth:
8 ounces Philadelphia cream cheese
Mix together:
4 green onions, tops included, chopped fine or coarse as you wish
1 green pepper, chopped into 1/4-inch pieces
1 sweet red pepper, chopped into 1/4-inch pieces
2 tablespoons green celery, chopped fine
Mix cheese and chopped vegetables. Spread on unbuttered bread just before serving, so that the bread will not get soggy.

sweets

DROP COOKIES

As the name implies, drop cookies
should be dropped from a spoon
then spread evenly with a rubber
spatula so they will rise evenly.
If this is not done they rise
up in the center more like small
cakes, and the right texture is
lost. It is also important,
when you are going to use the
cookie sheets or pans a second
time in your cookie-baking
session, that they have time to
cool off before the second batch
of cookies is dropped on them. If
they are the least bit warm the
cookies tend to melt before
they go into the oven, and this
will destroy the texture.

OATMEAL SESAME COOKIES

Mix together:
1/2 cup oil
1-1/2 cups dark-brown sugar

1 egg, well beaten
Combine and mix in:
2 tablespoons milk or buttermilk
1-1/4 cups rolled oats
1/2 cup raisins
3/4 cup sesame seeds (or sliced hazelnuts)
Sift together and mix in:
1-1/4 cups whole-wheat pastry flour
1/2 teaspoon baking soda
1/4 teaspoon salt
1/2 teaspoon nutmeg
1 teaspoon cinnamon
Drop from spoon dipped in cold water. Bake at 375°until brown.
Makes about 36 cookies

APPLESAUCE COOKIES

Cream together:
1/2 pound butter (at room temperature)
2 cups sugar
Add and beat in well:
1 egg
Mix together and beat in:
3 cups flour
1 teaspoon cinnamon
1/2 teaspoon powdered cloves
1/8 teaspoon salt
1 teaspoon baking soda
Add and stir in well:
1 cup unsweetened, thick applesauce
1 cup chopped walnuts
Drop on greased cookie sheet, spread with spatula and bake at 425° until brown.
Makes about 36 cookies

SOUR CREAM COOKIES

Cream together:
1/2 pound butter (at room temperature)
2 cups white sugar
Add and beat in well:
2 eggs
Then add and beat in:
1/2 pint sour cream
1 teaspoon baking soda
1 teaspoon vanilla
1/2 teaspoon powdered cardamon seed (optional)
1/2 teaspoon salt
When soft ingredients are well mixed, stir in:
4 cups sifted flour
Spoon onto greased cookie sheet and spread with spatula. Bake at 425° about 10 minutes. Remove from sheet to cool.
Makes about 36 cookies

sweets

MOLASSES COOKIES

The thought of these old-fashioned cookies, served hot with a glass of cold rich milk, wafts me back to a Midwestern farmhouse kitchen where hungry boys home from school made them disappear like magic.

Beat well together:

1 cup sugar
1/2 cup molasses
1/4 pound butter (at room temperature)

Add and beat in:

2 eggs

Then add and beat in:

1/2 cup sour milk or buttermilk
2 teaspoons baking soda

Add and mix in gently:

3 cups sifted flour
1/2 teaspoon baking powder
1 teaspoon salt
1 teaspoon cinnamon
1 teaspoon powdered ginger
1/4 teaspoon powdered cloves
1/2 cup raisins (optional)

Drop from spoon onto greased cookie sheet, spreading around with a spatula. Bake at 425° until done, perhaps 10 minutes. Remove immediately from sheet to cool.

Makes about 36 cookies

BANANAS FLAMBÉ

Mix Mix together over low heat:

1/2 cup fresh orange juice
rind of 1 orange, grated
1/2 cup water
2 tablespoons Benedictine
2 tablespoons curaçao
1 cup dark-brown sugar
1/4 teaspoon ground coriander seed
1/4 teaspoon fresh ground nutmeg

Heat this mixture only enough to dissolve the brown sugar.

Mix together:

1 teaspoon cream of tartar
4 cups water

Peel:

6 large firm bananas, with no brown spots

Dip peeled bananas into cream of tartar solution to keep them from turning dark. Drain them and then cut across and lengthwise to make 4 equal pieces of each banana.

Melt in a large frying pan, preferably copper clad:

4 tablespoons butter

Lay 1/2 of the banana pieces in skillet, cut side down. Fry until lightly brown, shaking skillet so they do not stick. Turn over and fry a little longer, but not until brown or they will fall apart; keep them whole. Before frying the rest of the bananas, melt in the skillet:

4 tablespoons more butter

When all bananas are fried, put them in a chafing dish or other dish that can be kept hot. Pour the hot orange mixture over them. You are now ready to flame the bananas. Warm gently over very low heat (do not overheat or the alcohol will evaporate):

1/2 cup brandy (flaming type preferably, with high percentage alcohol)

Pour warm brandy into small serving vessel that can be kept hot and place it and the chafing dish of bananas on the table. Turn off the lights—candlelight only for this. Light the brandy and immediately pour it over the bananas. If the banana mixture has been kept hot, the brandy will continue to burn as you serve each guest a flaming portion. All this is really not difficult to do, and is dramatic and extra delicious also. Just follow directions exactly as given, especially regarding temperatures.

Serves 6

SUGAR DROP COOKIES

Cream together:
2 cups sugar
1/2 pound butter (at room temperature)
Add and mix well together:
2 eggs, beaten lightly
Then stir in:
1 cup sour milk or buttermilk
Combine and mix in:
4 cups flour
1 teaspoon baking soda
1 teaspoon salt
1 teaspoon baking powder
1 teaspoon nutmeg
1/2 teaspoon vanilla
1 teaspoon caraway seeds (optional)
Drop from spoon on baking sheets, spread with spatula and bake at 350° until nicely brown.
Remove from sheet immediately and cool on wax paper.
Makes about 48 cookies

sweets

OLD-FASHIONED BOSTON CREAM PIE

Many years ago I ran a wholesale pie bakery in Columbus, Ohio, and of course developed and collected many, many pie recipes. Over the years some of these recipes were misplaced, among them this recipe. Without it I could not recreate the rich, delicious cake (for it really is a cake) that I remembered. Recently, I found the recipe. Here it is, one of those priceless, simple-but-wonderful recipes that good cooks love. Its uniqueness is the way in which the custard filling is made and how the eggs and sugar are combined.
Beat at high speed for 15 minutes (this is very important):
1 cup whole eggs, about 5 eggs, (at room temperature)
1 cup sugar

When eggs are whipped, sift into them this flour mixture:
(Measure the flour after sifting, then sift the dry ingredients together.)
1 cup plus 1 tablespoon sifted cake flour
1/4 cup sifted pie flour
1 teaspoon salt
1/4 teaspoon freshly ground nutmeg or cardamon seed
(It is necessary to have this mixture of cake and pie flour to get the right texture in the cake.)
When eggs and flour mixture have been completely combined, just mix in:
2 tablespoons milk (at room temperature)
1/2 teaspoon vanilla

Grease 2 cake pans, 1 9-inch and 1 8-inch. (This batter is not enough for 2 9-inch pans; too much for 2 8-inch ones.) Sift a little flour into the greased pans, shake it around and dump out the excess. This will insure that the cake comes out without sticking. Fill the tins and bake at 425° for about 12 minutes or until a straw comes out clean. Spread a dishtowel and sprinkle granulated sugar on it. Turn the cakes out on this. The sugar will keep them from sticking to the towel. When they are cool split each one into 2 layers with a sharp bread knife. Put the bottom half on a plate and spread on a generous amount of custard filling (recipe follows). Put on top layer of cake and sprinkle it with powdered sugar.
As a variation, spread on chocolate icing in place of the powdered sugar.
Makes 2 pies

CUSTARD FILLING
FOR BOSTON CREAM PIE

Mix in copper-clad pan so you
can boil without burning:
1-1/2 cups whole milk
3/4 cup sugar
Mix with wire whip and add to
hot milk; stir vigorously while
cooking until it thickens:
1 cup whole milk
3-1/2 tablespoons cornstarch
2 egg yolks
1/8 teaspoon salt
1 teaspoon vanilla
1 tablespoon Myers dark rum
(optional but excellent)
Also optional:
1 tablespoon grated lemon or
orange rind
1/8 teaspoon cardamon,
powdered
When thick remove from heat
and stir in:
1 tablespoon butter
Cool just enough so that filling
will not soak into the cake; then
spread before a scum forms on
the filling. There will be a bit
left over, but that is for the
cook to enjoy with a bit of cream

poured over it. Do not chill this
cake; chilling ruins the texture.
Serve immediately with plenty of
good hot coffee to go with it.

As a variation, prepare:
3 10-ounce packages frozen,
sugared red raspberries
defrosted only enough to get
most of the juice. Drain it off
and add enough water to make:
1 cup juice
Dissolve:
3 tablespoons cornstarch in
1/2 cup water
Add to juice and cook until
cornstarch clears. Pour immediately
over the raspberries. Stir gently
so as not to break up the berries
and set aside.
Whip together:
1/2 pint heavy cream
1/2 teaspoon vanilla
3 tablespoons powdered sugar
Pipe the whipped cream around the
edge of the cake and pile the
fruit in the center. Reserve a
dollop of whipped cream to
decorate the center. If any
whipped cream is left over it
goes with the custard to the cook.

sweets

FRESH FRUIT
MERINGUE SUPREME

Line a very large glass pie plate,
at least 12 inches, with brown
paper, making cuts around the
circle of paper so that it will
fit down into the plate.
Whip until the whites stand up
in peaks:
2/3 cup egg whites (5-6 eggs)
(Have whites at room temperature;
this is important.)
Add gradually, beating in gently
just until sugar is dissolved:
**1-1/4 cups plus 1/2 tablespoon
sugar**
When sugar is dissolved, fold
in gently:
3/8 teaspoon vanilla

Spread the meringue in the paper-lined pie plate, taking it up the sides to form a shell to hold the fruit. If your plate isn't large enough to use all of the mixture, make a smaller one, too. It will keep several days quite well.

Bake at 275° for at least 55 minutes. The shell needs to dry out thoroughly. When done, as soon as it is cool enough to handle, turn it over and pull off the paper. Let the meringue cool for at least 1 hour, then brush on the inside a thick coating of:

melted sweet chocolate

This will keep the fruit from soaking the meringue. Put into the refrigerator to chill for at least 1 hour.

Prepare 3 cups of whatever fresh fruit is available, but start with:

1 cup fresh pineapple

With a sharp knife cut off both ends, then stand the pineapple on end and slice down, turn and slice down again, until you have cut off all of the outside blossom remains. Split the fruit in half the long way, then split each half into long fourths. Stand each segment on end and slice off the core part. Lay each piece down and cut it into 1/8-inch pieces.

This is the easy way to prepare pineapple.

Mix together:

1/8 teaspoon powdered
cardamon seed
dash of nutmeg
dash of cinnamon
1 cup honey

Add this mixture to the pineapple and stir well. Peel and slice:

1 large or 2 small bananas

Mix with pineapple immediately; the honey will keep them from turning dark.

Peel and add:

fresh mandarin orange or
tangerine segments
other fresh fruit in season,
sliced or cubed

Let fruit marinate in the refrigerator for at least 1 hour to blend flavors.

Drain the fruit thoroughly then fill the meringue with it. Cover with:

whipped cream, sweetened

Garnish with:

fresh whole strawberries or
cherries

Serve thoroughly chilled, cutting the wedges with a sharp knife. As a variation, put a layer of custard in the meringue before adding the fruit. (See black bottom pie[page 178] for custard recipe.)

sweets

BLACK BOTTOM PIE

Years ago when I was traveling in
the South a friend took me to
a fine restaurant in Meridian,
Mississippi, where one of the
specialties of the house was this
delicious pie. Of course I asked
for the recipe and they readily
gave it to me. Several times since
I have found what purported to be
black bottom pie, but it certainly
wasn't the delicious dessert I had
in Meridian. Follow the recipe
faithfully and you will add to
your fame in the kitchen.
To make the crust, roll to
pulverize:
14 gingersnaps
Add and mix together to make an
even blend:
5 tablespoons melted butter
Line the bottom of a 9-inch pie
pan with this mixture, bake at
450° for 10 minutes and
allow to cool.

Put in a double boiler:
2 cups milk, scalding hot
Add and beat in well, one at
a time:
4 egg yolks
Combine and stir into milk and
egg mixture:
1-1/2 tablespoons cornstarch
1/2 cup sugar
Cook in the double boiler for
20 minutes or until it coats the
spoon; then take out 1 cup of the
custard and add to it:
1 square of bitter chocolate,
shaved fine
Beat this chocolate mixture well
as it cools.
When cool, spread it evenly
or the baked pie shell.

Dissolve:
1 tablespoon gelatin in
2 tablespoons cold water
Add gelatin mixture to custard in
the double boiler, mix and allow
to cool.
Mix together:
1/2 cup sugar
1/4 teaspoon cream of tartar
Beat until stiff:
4 egg whites
Beat sugar mixture into egg
whites only until dissolved, then
add and beat in:
2 tablespoons bourbon whiskey
Fold this mixture into the
remaining custard, mixing in
lightly but well, then spread it
over the chocolate custard.
Mix together and spread on pie:
1/2 pint heavy cream, whipped
1/3 cup powdered sugar
1/2 teaspoon vanilla
Garnish with long shavings of:
semi-sweet chocolate
Refrigerate before serving.

TENNESSEE CHILI JELLY

Our friends, the Bakers, invited us to dinner one evening and the first thing my eye lighted on at the table was a dish of jelly that had a lovely pink color. It was a special gift for this occasion, my hostess said, brought by the lady who helped to serve, and the recipe came from the hills of Tennessee. It had a special flavor, made from the juice of sweet red chilies, not hot, but unusual. Try it! Here is the recipe:

Chop and cook gently for about 10 minutes:
6 large red sweet peppers
6 cups water
When done, pour into a cloth bag and hang to drain overnight. Do not squeeze the bag or the juice will be cloudy. Next day make the jelly according to directions on a package of:
certo
using:
the drained juice

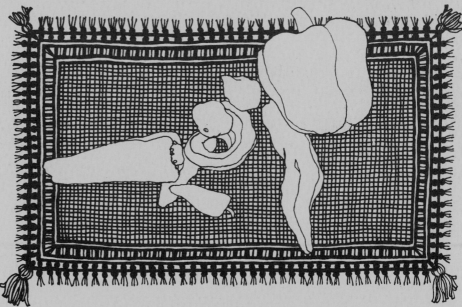

the pantry shelf

TURMERIC CORN RELISH

Put in boiling water and cook
for 2 minutes, counting only when
the water starts to boil again:
9 ears corn
Cut, then scrape the corn from
the cob.
Blend in a large bowl:
1 teaspoon turmeric
1 tablespoon dry ground mustard
2 teaspoons celery seeds
4 tablespoons salt
Pour in and stir until dry
ingredients are dissolved:
2 cups cider vinegar
1 cup light brown sugar
Mix in, then simmer gently for
30 minutes:
the corn kernels
3 cups minced fresh cabbage
1/2 cup chopped celery
2 small onions, minced
1 green pepper, minced
1 sweet red pepper, minced
Have hot sterilized jars ready;
fill and seal immediately.
Makes 5 or 6 pints

FRESH APRICOT CHUTNEY

In Ojai where we live, in
the late spring we can get
wonderful fresh non-irrigated
apricots, smaller in size than
the commercially grown ones so
that the flavor is concentrated.
With these we make chutney.
Cut in quarters but do not peel:
3 pounds apricots, slightly
on the green side
Add and cook until almost but
not quite soft:
3-1/2 pounds light brown sugar
4 cloves garlic, minced
1/2 red chili, Mexican type,
(not the small Japanese ones)
pounded or run dry in the
blender for 5 minutes until
chopped fine
1/4 pound fresh ginger root that
has been soaked, scraped and
sliced
(See recipe for ginger syrup,
this chapter.)
Add and cook for 30 minutes:
2-1/2 cups vinegar
1-1/2 pounds seedless raisins
2 teaspoons salt
1 teaspoon powdered cinnamon
1/6 teaspoon powdered cloves
1/6 teaspoon powdered cardamon
3/8 teaspoon cayenne pepper

Add after cooking:
1/2 cup fresh lemon or lime juice
This will give extra tartness
and fresh flavor.
This chutney will keep for months
in a covered crock and in
a cool place. But it won't last
that long if you let anybody
taste it!

ZOE SMITH'S CHILI SAUCE

This is an old Midwestern recipe.
Simmer slowly for 3 hours:
24 large, ripe tomatoes, chopped
4 onions, chopped
3 green peppers, chopped
4 tablespoons salt
1-1/2 cups vinegar
1-1/2 cups water
2 cups sugar
1 teaspoon allspice
1 teaspoon cloves, tied in
a cheesecloth bag
(remove when cooked)
Bottle immediately when
cooked. This will keep all winter.

PRESERVED WHOLE STRAWBERRIES

This recipe was given to me by a lady who many years ago escaped from Russia by way of Siberia to Japan and then to California.
Without cutting into the fruit, remove the hulls from:
1 cup large, firm, ripe strawberries
Gently toss berries in:
1 cup cane sugar
until they are coated. Repeat process 1 cup at a time. Let them stand overnight. Next day, heat the mixture in a pan large enough so that the mixture can spread out until it is not more than one berry deep. Bring to a gentle boil, shaking the pan gently. Do not stir or the skin of the berries will be broken. The boil should roll gently from the outside to the center of the pan. Boil for 2 minutes only. Again, let stand overnight, then bottle the berries and top them with paraffin. If this is done correctly, the berries will remain whole and plump and beautifully red in color.

GINGER SYRUP

Fresh ginger root has come on the market fairly recently. It should be put in water to soak overnight before cooking. This will allow it to absorb the moisture it has lost and make it easy to scrape away the outer skin and cut off any knobs. If it is to be used immediately it can be sliced or cubed or run through the blender to make a mush. To make a good sauce which will keep for weeks in a closed jar, scrape and dice into 1/4-inch cubes:
1 cup ginger root
Boil gently in:
4 cups water

Cook in a covered pan, boiling slowly for 1/2 hour without letting the water evaporate too much.
Drain off the liquid. Put 1 cup of it into a saucepan and add:
3 cups sugar
diced ginger root
1/2 cup corn syrup
Boil, covered, for 5 minutes—enough to make a simple syrup. This will make a thick syrup which can be added to many things. To make a thinner syrup use only 2 cups of sugar. A drop or 2 of green food coloring may be added.

BATTER FOR FRENCH FRYING VEGETABLES

Mix well together:
2 eggs
1/4 cup water
1/4 cup Kikkoman soy sauce
3/4 cup white flour
Coat cubed vegetables with this mixture and fry in deep fat. When golden brown, drain on paper towels and keep warm until ready to serve.

the pantry shelf

HUNGARIAN PEASANT NOODLES

Mix together, rubbing with spoon until thoroughly blended:
3 cups white flour
1 teaspoon herb salt*, or plain salt
1 teaspoon Calumet baking powder
1 sprig each, chopped: thyme, marjoram, costmary, basil, rosemary
Add and mix into dough:
1 tablespoon cooking oil
5 eggs, lightly beaten
Have ready large kettle of boiling, salted water. Put dough on bread board, rest board on side of kettle. Dip knife into boiling water, then cut off 1x1 inch piece of dough; dip knife again into kettle of water and dough will come off. Cook 1/3 of the dough at a time, allowing the noodles to cook 3 to 5 minutes, then drain and serve immediately. Doing it in this way will allow all of the noodles to cook approximately the same length of time.
Serves 8

CANNELLONI NOODLES

Mix together:
1-1/2 cups pastry flour
1 teaspoon salt
Make a well in the flour in a bowl and add:
9 egg yolks
Mix with a long fork, stirring the yolks into the flour and being careful not to spread the eggs on the sides of the bowl. Be sure the mixture is completely mixed; if in doubt, take it out of bowl and knead on a floured board until it feels smooth.

Alternate Method

I use a Kitchen Aid mixing machine and put the flour in the mixing bowl making a well in the flour. Then add the egg yolks carefully and by hand with the flat beater—not the wire whip—gently mix the flour and egg yolks. When it is rather well incorporated put the beater in the machine and finish the job. This gets all the egg yolks into the flour without losing any on the sides of the bowl.
Then turn dough out on a floured board and cut in in 4 even pieces. Pat it out elongated in size and with a rolling pin keep rolling it thinner and thinner. It should be as thin as paper, about 4-inches wide and very long. With a sharp knife cut across the long piece to the desired width you want the noodles. Let them dry in a wicker basket so they will have plenty of air circulation.
Boil them until done in salted water and then drain and wash them before serving.

COFFEE, STRONG AND SWEET

Many countries have their ways of serving coffee, most of them basically the same—rich, full bodied coffee and plenty of sugar. Here are three variations.

New Orleans You will need to get Luzianne brand coffee; it is in most markets or your grocer can get it without difficulty. The coffee can be made in your usual manner but very, very strong. And that is why you should have the Luzianne; it has chicory in it and therefore you can get a rich, heavy brew without having the triple dose of caffein which would probably make your heart do flip-flops. This strength is necessary because it is to be diluted, half coffee, half hot milk. Some say you only heat the milk; others say it must be brought to boil. Try it both ways. If you want to serve the coffee with real southern style, use two pots, one filled with milk and one with coffee, poured simultaneously into the cup.

Saigon Make a pot of coffee in your usual manner, but brewed double strength. When it is almost done add 1 heaping teaspoon sugar for each cup. Thoroughly dissolve the sugar before serving. Serve in mugs. In each mug put 1 stick cinnamon. Each guest can get the flavor he likes, then remove the cinnamon.

Turkey To make this coffee properly you need a regular Turkish pot. This is a deep, narrow-mouthed brass pot with a very long handle, long enough so that the pot can be safely lifted from the fire three times in the making. There is a tall bronze grinder available in specialty shops so the coffee can be freshly ground for éach pot.
For 2 people put into the pot:
1 cup cold water
3 tablespoons dark rich Columbia coffee, ground fine
2 tablespoons sugar
Bring to a good boil; it will come up in the pot with a scum or froth on top. Boil for 5 seconds. Remove from heat and let stand for 1 minute. Boil again 5 seconds, then let stand off the fire for a minute; do it a third time to a vigorous boil so that the scum rises right up to the top of the pot and pour it immediately into small cups, grounds and all. These repeated boilings will cause the grounds to settle and by the time it is cool enough to drink it will be clear.

coffee, tea, etc.

HERB TEAS

Ever since man discovered fire, he has used herbs and plants to make the liquid we know as tea, for pleasure and for medicinal purposes. All herbs have a medicinal effect; some are very mild and some are quite strong.

In making herb teas, the leaves of some plants are used, the seeds of others and the cut-up or powdered root of still others.

When the leaves or blossoms are used, it is only necessary to make an infusion by pouring boiling water over them in a preheated pot. When the stems are used, the tea should be steeped about 5 minutes. When the roots are used, they should be boiled for at least 15 minutes. Seeds make a stronger tea than the leaves and should be crushed and boiled 5 minutes. The infusion should be made extra strong, then thinned to taste by adding hot water when serving.

Interesting beverages may also be made by using regular teas— Indian, Chinese, Japanese or South American—as the base and then steeping with herbs. Various herbs may also be blended for unusual flavors. Combinations are available at health food stores. Following are some of the herbs which may be brewed into tea.

Angelica: Use the leaves.

Anise: Use the fresh leaves or crushed seeds; medicinally this is a relaxant, with a light licorice flavor.

Lemon Balm: Use the leaves and top stems; good hot or cold.

Orange Bergamot: Use the tops, about 1-foot long, and boil for a few minutes to extract all the flavor. One of the mint family, this is a classic tea of the American Indians. Serve hot or cold.

Borage: Use the leaves for unique flavor and medicinal value.

Burnet: Use the leaves, sparingly as a tea; some people do not like the cucumber-like fragrance.

Catnip: The leaves make an excellent tea; cats go wild for it.

Chamomile: Use the dried blossoms for relief from digestive upsets. Excellent and completely harmless.

Costmary: Use the leaves and boil slightly; it is very mild. According to many herbalists, this tea is a cure-all for many ills.

Fennel Seed: Use the crushed seeds. Serve hot or cold.

Flax: Cut a whole grapefruit into thin slices. Put skin, pulp and juice into 2 quarts water and 4 tablespoons flax seeds. Bring to boil and boil slowly for 15 minutes, then strain. To relieve cold symptoms, drink 1/2 cup every 2 hours.

Geranium: Use the leaves of the lime, lemon, rose, nutmeg or peppermint varieties. All make excellent teas.

Horehound: The root, boiled and made into a syrup, is an effective, but slightly bitter cough medicine.

Lavender: Use the sprigs for an exotic tea.

Linden: In Zurich, the fragrance of the linden blossoms in June is almost overpowering. The dried blossoms with their leaves make the most fragrant of all the teas, The addition of a little honey makes it extraordinary.

Lovage: Use the leaves and stems; serve hot or cold for a refreshing tea with a celery-like flavor. An old-fashioned medicinal.

Mints: Use the leaves and stems and boil slightly. Of the many varieties of mint, the apple, orange, peppermint, spearmint, pineapple and licorice types all make excellent teas.
Serve hot or cold.

Parsley: Use the leaves and stems and steep longer than most teas; a delicious drink and especailly nourishing because of the high quality protein contained in parsley.

Saffron: For its fragrance, many Dutch people add a pinch of saffron to their ordinary tea. The orange stigmas, steeped, are also served as a medicinal tonic.

Sage: The leaves of the ordinary, pineapple, black or variegated varieties may be used. All are good, but strong flavored.

Thyme: Use the top sprigs. Lemon thyme leads the list for flavor, but the garden, nutmeg, French, golden or silver varieties also make acceptable teas.

Verbena, Lemon: Use the leaves. This tea is very good and may be served with almost any type of meal at any time of day.

Woodruff, Sweet: Use the sprigs. This herb imparts the flavor to the German May Wine, but it also makes an excellent tea.

index

index

index

index

index

about the author

Alan Hooker, is the owner of the distinguished Ranch House restaurant in Ojai, California, the author of "Vegetarian Gourmet Cookery" and a long-time vegetarian. Thus some readers may be surprised to find the large sections of meat, fish and poultry recipes in this book. These were developed by Mr. Hooker during the period when the Ranch House converted from a pure vegetarian menu to an all-inclusive selection of dishes. Subsequently, he returned to the vegetarian diet personally, although his restaurant is noted for its unusual meat and seafood dishes.

A non-conformist and a self-taught cook, Alan Hooker began experimenting with the use of herbs to give zest and flavor to vegetarian dishes. When he began to create fish and meat dishes, he based these primarily on the use of herbs also, rather than on the traditional stock pot. Seventy-five of the herbs used in the Ranch House cuisine are grown in its garden.

Mr. Hooker's interest in food dates back to his childhood when his family lived next door to a retired chef from the Waldorf Astoria, who introduced Alan and his family to the world of international haute cuisine. In college he majored in chemistry, learning laboratory disciplines which were later helpful in formulating recipes and understanding the chemistry of food. After college he joined a traveling jazz band as a pianist and played at many of the great hotels and clubs in the United States and Europe; when not at the piano, Alan was likely to be found in the kitchen observing the chef, constantly adding to his culinary knowledge.

In spite of this background, Alan Hooker's professional involvement with food came almost by accident. He left the entertainment world to live in Ohio, on a commune engaged in the serious study of Eastern philosophy. In Columbus, he was offered a job as a pie salesman for a new bakery, but he said he would rather be in the kitchen making pies. Hired, he developed numerous pie crusts and fillings for the bakery and eventually managed it.

When the bakery made plans to expand into a chain, Alan left and with his wife Helen moved to Ojai, California. Here they opened a vegetarian boarding house where Alan did the cooking. Boarders brought guests and the food became so popular that the Hookers expanded into a restaurant, The Ranch House. In those days, however, the vegetarian diet was not so popular as it is today, and to make ends meet, the fish, fowl and meat dishes which appear in this book were added to the menu.

Ever curious and ever learning about food, Mr. Hooker has traveled widely throughout the world, sampling the cuisines of many countries, often in the finest restaurants where he inevitably ends up in the kitchen for a chat with the chef and leaves with a recipe.